ALW
BEING
READY!

Doug Harris

REACHOUT TRUST

BUILDING A BRIDGE OF REASON

Original edition first published by Kingsway Publications Ltd
1996 under the title "Open the Door"

This revised and updated edition published 2004
by Reachout Trust, 24 Ormond Road, Richmond,
Surrey TW10 6TH

ISBN 0 9513632 7 1

978-0-951363-27-0

Unless otherwise indicated, Scripture quotations are
from the *New American Standard Bible* (NASB)
© The Lockman Foundation 1960, 1962, 1963, 1968,
1971, 1972, 1973, 1975, 1977.

British Library Cataloguing Data
A catalogue record for this book is available
from the British Library

Contents

Section 4

Overview of what some Cults Believe

Introduction

When we first published this book in 1996, there was some debate over its title; in the end we settled for *Open the Door* because that is what we wanted people to do. However, as this Introduction shows, something needs to happen before we open the door: we need to get ready. 1 Peter 3:15 indeed shows we are always to be ready:

> **"But sanctify Christ as Lord in your hearts, always being ready to make a defence to every one who asks you to give an account for the hope that is in you, yet with gentleness and reverence."**

Surely that is impossible! No, because being ready is a process and the clock doesn't start ticking until you know that you are not ready - then you get ready. It will also be a process, different for each one of us. If my wife and I are due to leave home at 6 and she is not getting ready at 5 – we're late. That's not being nasty to my wife; that is living with her for 30+ years. She takes an hour to get ready, but I – 5 minutes before we leave - splash water on my face and put on the clean shirt!

We are all different and so the process for getting ready will be different. We also do not need to feel guilty if we cannot answer the first time we are challenged by the cult member, but the clock starts ticking and we need to put in the time to get ready.

Seated in a comfortable armchair watching top class athletes break world records makes it appear so easy. Out of the starting blocks and a mere ten seconds later it's all over and fame and fortune await the victor.

The reality, of course, is very different. When they arrive at the start line and are called to their marks, that is not the beginning. They would not be ready without months or even years of training for that one moment. Preparation for the day

5

that they can look back on with great satisfaction takes time and commitment.

As with breaking world records, witnessing to the cults and sharing Jesus with them does not come easy for most people. If you feel that you can simply walk to the 'starting blocks' and just have a go, this book is not for you. This book is for the hundreds of Christians I have met all over the country, who have confided that they do not find it easy to open their front doors and to share Jesus with those in the cults. I have spoken to thousands of people over the past 20+ years in seminars from Inverness to Truro, and from Southend to Swansea. The joy I have is in knowing that many of them are today reaching out to the cults in love. Many have found that with the right training they are ready not only to open the door, but also to lead cult members into the Kingdom of God.

I remember answering the phone one day to hear, in a voice full of jubilation, 'It works!' I suspected that this was a new way of selling double glazing or life insurance but intrigued I asked the obvious question – 'What works?' It turned out that the lady on the phone had been at one of my seminars a few weeks before. Just that day she had had the opportunity to put the teaching into practice. She had never managed to talk sensibly with the Jehovah's Witnesses at the door until then, and she was so excited. There are no five-year guarantees but I can assure you that there are many others who will confirm that it *does* work.

But it will take commitment. The cults are aware of this and spend much time in training. Sadly, Christians do not seem quite so bothered. Our attitude reminds me of my youngest son Luke – many years ago now – who could not say the word "seminar" and, when I returned from one particular weekend away, he asked me, "How did the cinema go?" It struck me after a while that this was almost prophetic of many of us Christians. We pay our money, watch the main event taking place up front, and maybe even feel some emotion for a while. However, when it is all over, we leave and nothing lasting has really affected us. Next week we need to do it all over again!

Know your enemy

Paul tells us that we are not to be ignorant of Satan's devices (2 Cor 2:11). Verses like this make me sit up and take notice. I know the content of the verse is forgiveness — if we do not forgive then Satan will have a foothold — but there are many other devices of Satan and sometimes we are only too ignorant of them.

Ephesians 6:11 adds to this that we are to stand firm against the schemes of the devil. How can we stand firm against the schemes if we do not know what they are? The area of the cults is one of Satan's major schemes, as we will discover in chapters 1–5. Through varying degrees of spiritual intensity and subtly changing doctrines, he brings many into his domain. We need to know about his schemes so that we can both be protected ourselves and help those who may be involved.

Much modern warfare and fight against evil, such as drug smuggling, is based on intelligence about the enemy. Even in Biblical times, warfare was carried out by seeking to get an assessment of the enemy first. The spies in Joshua's days had a human frame and as such were very vulnerable. The spies today fly high in the sky at hundreds of miles per hour, but both do the same job. How can we have any hope of resisting if we do not know where he is coming from? Unless we have some idea of how he will react when we move forward, we do not know what to do for the best. We should certainly not spend hours concentrating on Satan but we should at least know what the Bible reveals about him and what effect that has on us today.

The Bible shows Satan, among other things, as a deceiver (Rev.12:9); as the one who causes doubt in God (Gen.3:1-5). A liar, indeed the father of lies (Jn.8:44). The tempter (Mt.4:1) and, if he is allowed to be, a devourer (1 Pet.5:8). We must understand and be aware of how all this affects our Christian life.

I attended a large Christian meeting a few years ago where a well-known controversial speaker was in full flow. "We don't need all these anti-cult groups; we just need to preach Jesus," his voice rang out. Why did he say that? I suspected then, and have had no cause to change my mind since, that it was to defend his own position and to make sure that no one checked on his teaching. However, there are those whose ministry is not just anti-anything but a positive calling as 'watchmen' within the body of Christ. They are not there to criticise everyone who does not hold their views on, for instance, the return of Christ. Nor are they there to find a demon under every new preacher's notes. They are there to give a warning to the body of Christ where teaching or action is not Biblical. Reachout Trust, I believe, has been called to be a help to the body of Christ in this area.

People have accused Reachout Trust of being a 'negative' ministry. My answer is always the same 'tongue-in-cheek' reply: "If sharing Jesus in a relevant way is negative, then I agree with you." What we are doing is not negatively saying someone is wrong, but positively showing them there is something and indeed Someone better.

This book will not provide you with scare stories of those who have been involved in hideous cults, or testimonies of 'great escapes'. This is not the purpose of the book. What we are aiming to provide is an overview of what you are likely to find behind the public face of your town. From this, each of us will be better prepared both to pray and to warn young or ignorant Christians of the dangers. Most importantly, we will be ready to be used as messengers of the love of God to the people caught up in these areas.

Know your faith

Chapters 6–10 will help make sure we know our own position in Christ. This section is the heart of the book. Here we will look at building ourselves up in our own faith. These chapters are the 'meat' in the sandwich. Without this section we have nothing to get our teeth into; we cannot help others if we do not have a firm foundation ourselves.

The two greatest excuses - or occasionally genuine concerns - for not talking with people involved in the cults are ignorance and fear. Ignorance of what the cults believe will be covered in the final section. A positive knowledge of what we believe must come first and this will be covered especially in chapters 9–10. British ambassadors abroad always need to know what the government is thinking and doing in Westminster. Without constant briefing, they would be communicating their own ideas and not being the representatives of Britain. It is no different when we are ambassadors of heaven in a foreign land on earth. We need constant briefing from the Lord to know what He is thinking and doing. This way we will be representing Him and not just our own ideas.

This section will also help deal with any fear. Most have a fear of being beaten in a 'Bible-bashing' contest. Many, too, have a fear of looking a fool for not knowing an answer or, even worse, being convinced by the argument of the cult. These fears are, of course, brought on by the one who is the author of fear: the devil. Knowing the One Whose love casts out that fear, and knowing the Word ourselves are the basis for our sharing without trepidation. These chapters are not a complete guide to theology but they will give an excellent beginning. Learning from God is a daily ongoing experience.

Know the cults

The way we express what we know is also vital; we are not called on to Bible-bash. 'Wimbledon-witnessing' produces little, if any, effect. The Christian serves his best text that is almost an ace. Somehow the cult member dashes across the baseline and returns the ball with interest. The top-spin almost fools the Christian and he finds himself on the defensive, and on it goes. Occasionally someone scores a point, but we seem always to return to deuce and no one ever wins the match. This, as we shall see, is not the way to win these people to Christ. If, however, we are firmly anchored in the Scriptures, I do not think there is any need to pretend we are on the Centre Court at Wimbledon. We can take a calm approach to the subject being discussed and ask questions rather than just firing accusations at 100 mph.

Chapters 11 onwards will give an overview of the beliefs and lifestyle of several well-known cults as well as some ideas about how to approach them. They will also give Biblical refutation to some of the most used arguments of the cults. This form of witnessing will probably be more akin to running the marathon than the 100 metres – the quality of staying-power is usually necessary with the cults. We trust this book will go a long way to getting you in shape.

There will be other groups that are not mentioned here and you will probably have more questions. Reachout Trust is a ministry that is here to help individual Christians and churches in any way we can. Do not hesitate to ring or write and we will try to provide the information you require.

SECTION 1
OVERVIEW OF CULTS

1 - What is a Cult?

Few of us who saw the events concerning the Branch Davidians in the Spring of 1993 could remain unmoved. On April 19 nearly 80 people were burnt to death in a small town in Texas that most of us had never heard of, but Waco became the talking point for Christians and non-Christians alike. In the early days many started calling it "Wacky-Waco". At the beginning of the siege no one had the full knowledge of the tragedy that was to follow and such jokes seemed appropriate. Looking back on the events that followed, we would not be quite so ready to make light of the people and places involved.

Most of us probably think that the term 'cult' is typified by Waco or Jonestown or Heaven's Gate or any of the tragic cases of lives being laid down at the command of the group leader. However, these are the extreme cases and maybe we need to be a little more conservative in our thinking and use of the word cult.

Meaning of the word 'cult'

First we must define our terms. What is a cult? Chambers' *English Dictionary* defines it as:

> "A system of religious belief: formal worship: a sect: an unorthodox or false religion: a great, often excessive, admiration for a person or idea: the person or idea giving rise to such admiration."

Always Being Ready!

The *Concise Oxford Dictionary* agrees that it is:

> "A system of religious worship esp. as expressed in ritual ... devotion or homage to a person or thing ... a popular fashion esp. followed by a specific section of society."

Collins' *English Dictionary* probably gives the most comprehensive definition that adds a little to what has been noted above:

> "A specific system of religious worship, esp. with reference to its rites and deity. 2. a sect devoted to the beliefs of a religious or other cult. 3. a group having an excessive ideology and ritual practices centred on sacred symbols esp. one characterised by lack of organisational structure. 4. intense interest in and devotion to a person, idea or activity. 5. the person. idea, etc. arousing such devotion."

As these definitions show, in the strict sense of the original word, almost any group that meets for a specific religious purpose could be called a cult. However, modern day usage has taken on the more specific meaning that comes out in the secondary definition. This is summed up in such phrases as an 'excessive ideology', 'intense interest in and devotion to a person', and 'an unorthodox or false religion'.

You will find disagreement among the 'experts' about the definition of a cult; indeed some would want to class a number of the groups mentioned in this book as sects. They would also want to use terms such as New Religious Movements. The main reason seems to be the overuse of the word 'cult' and its use in extreme situations.

I will use the word 'cult' not in a 'nasty' sense, but it seems to sum up the variety of groups that we deal with. The majority of such groups use some form of poor copy of the mainstream evangelical gospel; I will therefore give a two-part definition to the word 'cult'. The first part covers such groups described above and the second covers most groups that are secular in nature. The application of these definitions will become apparent as you move through the book.

Definition of a cult

A group whose message includes either the need of a spiritual change now, or gives a hope of eternal salvation, or encourages a relationship with God, without the reality of repentance from sin and acceptance of Jesus Christ as God the Son and Saviour.

Groups who employ methods of strict authoritarianism, or mind control, or insist that their group is the only true one, or who hold the threat of expulsion for any who do not accept leadership decisions without question.

We will discover some groups who, although they do not fall down on the first area of theology, do on the second section regarding method. There will also be other groups who will sometimes show cultic tendencies without being a cult in the strict sense of the word. We will seek to make these distinctions clear when talking about specific groups.

While on definitions we should mention the biblical one found in 2 Corinthians 11:4:

> "... another Jesus whom we have not preached, or you receive a different spirit which you have not received, or a different gospel which you have not accepted ..."

Another Jesus, a different spirit and a different gospel. These three descriptions of the teaching of false apostles will be used to sum up three different groupings of cults we have today. However, we also see in this chapter the 'angel of light' syndrome, the disguise that Satan uses so often. Master forgers spend years perfecting their art for the £20 and £50 notes but we never read stories of someone taking years to perfect a forged £3 note. The reason is obvious – Satan is the same; he only ever counterfeits that which exists and is of value. We should not be surprised, therefore, to see the cults mimicking much of Christian belief and lifestyle.

Test of a cult

Just as the Bank of England has its methods of detecting forgeries we too can often detect who is a cult by using the following tests. However, most of the method deals with checking the *original* in great detail and not the forgery – this is a lesson for us.

Use or misuse of Scripture

Are portions of Scripture left out to give half-truths or the meaning of a verse twisted to suit pet doctrines? Are verses taken out of the context of the chapter or of the rest of Scripture? Most false doctrines of the cults can be detected by a simple look at the context. An example is the Mormon claim that the two joined rods of Ezekiel 37:15ff are the Bible and the Book of Mormon. The Bible clearly shows us that these rods are not books but two parts of Israel that will be reunited. The interpretation of the Latter-day saints is twisting Scripture out of context.

Another area that many cults will use here is majoring on minor issues. The Jehovah's Witness will want to spend much time talking about the shape of the piece of wood on which Jesus was nailed but miss the importance of what He accomplished there.

The person of Christ

Jesus is not just a prophet or a good man. He is God and a right relationship with Him is vital for salvation. Cults will nearly always downgrade Jesus and His work, and to combat this we will discuss in other chapters the revelation of Jesus given by the Bible.

Is salvation earned?

Salvation only comes through Jesus Christ and is a free gift; it cannot be earned. By it we are delivered from the domain of Satan into the Kingdom of Christ. Nothing human beings do can achieve this. However, if you have downgraded Jesus and His work, the uplifting of man becomes vital. Man must do what Christ has not done.

Most cults teach that, in one way or another, you must work for salvation and need to keep the laws and ordinances of the group beyond the acceptance of Jesus Christ. We will return to this vital matter later in the book.

Exclusiveness

Most cults believe that they are the only ones bringing salvation. The moment you detect anything that appears to say, 'Our group is the only way to God', beware, because they are most likely a cult. Some people only find out too late when they try to leave the group. The use of emotional pressure is often applied with the implication that leaving the particular group means leaving the hope of salvation behind.

Unique/Special Revelation

Many cults will claim special revelation that only they have. This is the old heresy of Gnosticism or, as a friend of mine calls it, the 'Esoteric Doughnut'.

This simply means there is some hidden knowledge that you can only get by joining the group – you must be initiated in order to receive the revelation. The doughnut is the sugary one with jam in the middle that you do not see until it covers your shirt front. Looking from the outside all you see is the sugar, but for the initiated there is the jam in the middle.

Always Being Ready!

Be wary of any group or individual that says they have a special unique revelation through dream, prophecy or whatever, if it cannot be checked out against the clear teaching of Scripture.

Domination

Whenever one person takes charge of a group to control its every movement, you will more often than not witness the formation of a cult. It is, of course, just possible that every decision the leader takes is of God and so the group would follow in God's way, but most Christian leaders would not want to be in the isolated situation that many cult leaders achieve. As we shall see, this area is also the one that produces most cultic tendencies in otherwise Christian groups.

Just before we return to draw some important lessons from Waco and the events surrounding David Koresh and the Texas compound, we need to underline an important fact. Most people involved in the cults are there for genuine reasons. Some Christians feel that we should not bother with these people because they have made up their own mind to turn their back on God. The truth is that the majority of people have not made a conscious decision to turn from God. The person in the cult is searching for the truth and has been misled. Our response should be one of love, compassion and understanding, not hatred and judgement.

Lessons from Waco

Desire to know God better

In the weeks after Waco, in the many media programmes I was invited on, I met some of the relatives of those that had died in Waco. However, what became clear is that when David Koresh first presented his message, in 1992, to the students of the Seventh-Day Adventist Bible Schools, it was not as the 'sinful Messiah', as he later called himself. His message was that he could help them understand the

Scriptures better and thus know the Lord in a deeper way. He felt that he had a special message to take to the Adventist churches and was fulfilling a God-given commission. For hour after hour Koresh recited Scripture from memory and wove together a message of impending doom and a way of escape for the few. For some, the message was convincing and they followed Koresh, not to join a cult but to serve the Lord and be His true people in the last days up to and through Armageddon.

This may be difficult for many to understand, but we have the benefit of hindsight. Today, as people go through the traumas of life – bereavement, marriage break-up, violence – they became vulnerable to the first message of any convincing hope that comes along. Do not be quick to condemn such people; first find out the circumstances that have led them into the cult. Remember that most cult members are sincere people. They believe in what they are saying. To those without hope the cults hold out the apparent goal of knowing God.

Twisting of Scripture

If there is one counterfeit ploy that the devil appears to delight in using more than any other, it is the twisting of God's words. He started that way in the Garden of Eden and he continued when he tempted the Lord in the wilderness. He does not always tell outright lies – half-truths can sometimes be more effective. 'You shall not die', was true, but only half the truth. The Father would certainly have given the angels charge to minister to Jesus, but again that was only part of the truth.

Koresh, however, took Scriptures and wove them in such a way that black ended up white. He became the 'sinful Messiah' – a complete contradiction in terms. However, he quoted many Scriptures; surely the Bible cannot lie? The Bible indeed cannot lie but false apostles can take Scriptures out of context to make them say something else. I've heard, for example, that because John 1:1 says that Jesus was the

'Word', and a word is simply an expression of a thought, it is obvious Jesus had no pre-existence. He was simply a thought in the mind of God. Again, we read in 1 Thessalonians 4:16 that Jesus will return with the voice of an archangel. Who alone has the voice of an archangel? Well then, Jesus must be an archangel. These statements may seem logical but they are not borne out when the whole of Scripture is put together. This we mentioned earlier, and we will return to it in a later chapter, because it is the crucial test.

The only way

Often linked to the last point is the proof, from Scripture, that a particular group is the only way. There are literally scores of groups in Britain today who are claiming this. Along with Scripture twisting, they will use direct revelation and the historical evidence of the group. Once someone believes that this group is the only channel that God is using today and that its leader or leaders have direct access to God, the rest is simple.

Koresh was the Messiah, the one who would lead the remnant through the final battle of Armageddon. He was special; he was the only one who could understand and open the seven seals of Revelation chapters 5-8. This proved that he had access to God's way and plan more than anyone else on earth at the time.

Powerful, domineering personality

Most groups have such people. Koresh was a charismatic character who could preach for hours and, either through his skill at communicating or people's fear of reprisals, could hold his audience captivated. He was not afraid to use threats of violence if his natural personality did not work.

Many cults hold their members by fear or threats. Either the fear that if they leave the group, they will leave their only hope of salvation, or the threat of expulsion and being cut off from the rest of their family and friends. Or even the threat of physical violence. In this way, cults hold their members and dominate them and their lives.

The various dictionary definitions of 'authoritarianism' seem to sum up what we are talking about here:

> "Setting authority above liberty. Dictatorial." – Chambers' *20th Century Dictionary*

> "Favouring, denoting or characterised by strict obedience to authority. Favouring, denoting or relating to government by a small elite with wide powers." – Collins' *English Dictionary*

> "Favouring, encouraging or enforcing strict obedience to authority, as opposed to individual freedom. Tyrannical or dom- ineering." – *Concise Oxford Dictionary*

> "Of, relating to, or favouring blind submission to authority. Of, relating to, or favouring a concentration of power in a leader or an elite not constitutionally responsible to the people." – Webster's *New Collegiate Dictionary*

These definitions lead us to see that an authoritarian, dom- ineering leadership will have wide-ranging powers but not be responsible to anyone. It will always want to see that its authority is obeyed without question and will have little regard for the individual. It will want to dominate rather than serve.

Mind control

One question often asked over Waco was, "How can ordinary, rational people put themselves in such a situation?" The answer is probably best summed up by the words: 'mind control'. These were 'buzz words' at the time of Waco, but what do they really mean? A simple analogy is that of a computer program. Under normal circumstances every time you hit the letter 'a' on the keyboard an 'a' is produced on the screen. Supposing, however, someone rewrites the program so that every time you type 'a', 'b' will appear on the screen, 'b' will produce 'c' and so on. It will happen automatically and there is nothing you can do about it until the offending program is rewritten. That is what happens to someone under mind control. Normal responses cease to exist and a new set of reactions occur. How it is done, however, is not always as easy as writing a new computer program.

With Koresh several factors were involved. Sleep deprivation, bad diet, lack of free time, hour after hour of the same teaching – all conspired to cause the classic zombie-like response. The will has been broken and has been supplanted by the will of someone else. Not every group, however, goes to such draconian lengths. Sometimes it is as easy as just making sure you only read the material the group wants you to.

Take, for instance, the group that weekly reads a book to you. The book is written from the cult's viewpoint and is liberally sprinkled with Scripture quotations. First, a paragraph of the book is read. Next a question is asked, constructed by the group, to bring out a particular aspect of the teaching in their book. Third, you answer the question constructed by the group, with the words written by the group, in the book that explains what the group believes. Add to this the group's belief that all individual thinking is of the devil and that the only truth is in the group not in an individual, and the result is that a rational individual comes to think what the group thinks and speak as the group speaks. This is a description of the training of a Jehovah's Witness, not an extreme new cult.

Mind control in most cults, should not be thought of as 'torture' but basically only providing a percentage of the truth. The individual will make a rational decision based on the information provided – present them with all the facts and they may make a very different decision.

For instance, you read in a company brochure that in 2003 their figures were the best in the world when compared with all those in the same field. Your decision is to invest in such a firm. However, what you are not told is that in 2004, several members of the board were charged with fraud and the accountant was convicted of misrepresenting the facts. With this knowledge a different decision would be reached.

New light

A further characteristic of a cult must always be the ability to bring 'new light' to the group. It must be clearly documented from Scripture and show why they now believe it even if it contradicts something they believed last week. Every group has its ways of progressive revelation so that they can keep up with the times and alter any false prophecies or pronouncements from the past.

David Koresh went through several changes until he pronounced that he was the Messiah. Each change was a new revelation from God and a new understanding of His word.

Friend/enemy syndrome

As I have watched programmes and read the reports concerning David Koresh and the aftermath of Waco in the years since those events, one thing in particular has struck me, and that is the number of people who still believe in David Koresh as the Messiah, and that he will rise again. However, these were people who lost all their family in the fire, and were on trial for their lives. This has highlighted to me what was one of the strongest messages from Waco.

The Branch Davidian compound had a literal boundary and you were either in or out. Every cult has that boundary somewhere in its teaching. It may not be a literal compound but it will be mental or spiritual. Everyone on the inside of that boundary line is a friend. They would never hurt me or harm me. They would never tell me a lie. I can trust them totally.

Conversely, everyone outside that line is an enemy. Their sole purpose is to take me away from the truth. They will deceive me and tell me lies and every action is intended to harm me.

Always Being Ready!

When the federal authorities moved in to end the siege, this was the enemy coming to persecute and harm. The US authorities revealed in their news conference what they believed would happen. When they moved in to knock holes in the wall and insert gas, all the mothers would grab their children and run out. We now know, however, just how the Davidians acted: instead of coming out they moved further in. This attitude is found in every cult. If we persecute them and put pressure on them, all we will accomplish is to push them further in to the false teaching.

Reaching such people

These are some of the main characteristics of cults that we can glean from David Koresh and the Branch Davidians. Before we close this chapter, however, and seek to give four different groupings for cults, I believe we must show how to react to such people.

In John's gospel, chapter 4, we have the story of Jesus' meeting with the woman of Samaria by the well. This passage gives the key to how we are to act in these circumstances.

We are told in verse four that Jesus had to pass through Samaria. No self-respecting Jew would do that, but Jesus did. Why? For one woman who, in the world's eyes, was no good and did not deserve to hear any message of hope. The Jews had condemned the Samaritans, who were a 'cult' in their day; many if not all her neighbours had condemned this woman: she was an outcast of the outcasts. Tragically, this attitude of condemnation is one that many Christians have towards the cults. On what scriptural basis do we condemn them to hell without giving them the chance to hear the gospel of grace, possibly for the first time? Does God not love the Jehovah's Witness at the door, or the Moonie in the High Street, or even the witch in the coven? John 3:16 has no exceptions in my Bible. God loves *all* the world, including those in the cults.

When I wrote the book, *Don't Close the Door*, I put this on the back cover:

> "For God so loved the world, except Jehovah's Witnesses and Mormons, that He gave His only begotten Son, that whoever, providing they are not associated with the Watchtower Society or the Latter-day Saints, believes in Him should not perish, but have eternal life. So, it would appear, reads the Bible of many Christians."

Many people picked the book up and laughed at that, but it is not really a laughing matter. It is amazing to me that we pray for missionaries working among the 'heathen' with their other gods and a different Jesus. But we will not talk to the person in the same position on our doorstep. Maybe it is easier to pray for someone a thousand miles away than talk to the person standing two feet in front of us.

Not only does God love: John 3:17 clearly shows that Jesus did not come to judge or condemn. Judgement will come in the end, but for now we are still living in the day of grace. What scriptural right do we have to condemn? None. Indeed, we are clearly being disobedient to God's Word if we do so. Why is it that the moment we meet cult members all we want to do is tell them how wrong and rotten they are? Jesus could have acted the same way to that woman. He knew all about her and could have pointed the finger and exclaimed, "You adulteress!" Instead He asks her for a drink of water. The woman is puzzled because Jews have no dealings with Samaritans. Jesus has begun to build a bridge of love and trust to the woman. He has caused her to wonder, because this is not how He was supposed to have acted.

Cult members have been told how Christians will react. When we do what is expected and attack and condemn, we are forcing them into the cult. When we love and show interest in them as people, it puts a question mark in their life and another piece of the bridge is built.

Always Being Ready!

Jesus now goes a step further with the woman. He does not even begin with the woman but begins to show her that He has something that she does not have: the water that will quench her thirst forever. She came to the well to get the 'dead' water but Jesus talks about 'living' water. He compares the 'copy' she has with His 'original'. It is the way to share with cult members: they believe that they are in the only true church; why should they change? The only reason they will leave is if they see something better in us. First we sow the question mark and then we put in the positive reasons. The woman's interest was roused by Jesus' attitude and words, and she was then willing to talk.

Jesus still had to deal with what was wrong in the woman's life. He had clear knowledge, given by the Holy Spirit, of just how sinful she was, but notice how it was worked out in love. It's almost as if Jesus said, "We're having such a great conversation; why don't you go and get your husband so he can join in?" No accusation but a question that went to the very root of the woman's problem. Learn from Jesus: a question is always better than an accusation.

The woman knew her life was wrong; she knew that Jesus had something she did not have; she knew His attitude towards her was one of love and care. Later she would go home, knowing that something was different but not sure exactly what. A big question mark had been sown in her heart that would bear fruit.

Not every cult member we talk to will come to Christ, but I believe that in most cases we can sow the doubt and then let the Holy Spirit do His job. We have not been called to 'save people' – indeed, we cannot – but we have been called to communicate the message of salvation, by grace and not by works. Our job is to communicate; God's job is to save.

2 - 'Another Jesus' Cults

Using the phrases from 2 Corinthians 11:4, we will highlight three different groups of cults. There will be some overlap and some groups could appear in more than one section.

The first group of cults is best summed up by the phrase: 'another Jesus'. The name implies that they are close to Christianity, and they will often use the same phrases as Christians. There are some who only have to hear the word 'Jesus', and they will want to believe that the group is Christian. Note carefully that there will be those preaching another Jesus. The name stays the same but the characteristics and the achievements are different. At first glance it may appear real, but under closer examination we can detect a forgery.

As a side issue, this underlines for us the importance of language. Genesis 11:1 tells us that the people before Babel used both the same language and the same words. They did not just have the same language but used the words with a particular meaning. They understood each other perfectly because they knew in what context a word was used. When we use words, for instance, 'sin', it leaves our lips but in our minds stays the specific definition we are using for that word. When it arrives in the ears of the hearer, they do not have our definition and so supplant their own, which may be totally different from what we intended. One word, two or more different meanings - just as "biscuit" and "jelly" have a different meaning in the 'common' language of Britain and America. We must ensure that even common words are explained carefully and that we leave no room for the supplanting of a different meaning.

Counterfeit paintings can fool some people. Imagine that you were offered a genuine Rembrandt or Picasso and a very good copy, side by side. If you were not an expert there is only a 50–50 chance that you would choose the right one. However, supposing you knew exactly which was which when you were offered them. There is no question that you would choose the original for its value, whether you liked the painting or not.

This is often the position in which that people who join these cults are placed. The masterpiece is represented by the message and person of the real Jesus. The counterfeit is represented by the message and organisation of the cult. Many people have never heard about the real Jesus or, if they have, did not respond at the time. Now in a moment of crisis they cry out to God to help them. A few days later there is, as they think, God's answer on the doorstep. They hear about Jesus and God and about being saved. This *must* be right. They have nothing to compare it with and their eye is not expert enough to detect the flaws. They accept the counterfeit and believe it to be true.

Our job, therefore, is to hold up the real and allow them to compare it with the counterfeit. I remember seeing an original Monet - we had a print of it at home - and there was no comparison between the two. Even if up until that day I had been convinced what I had at home was the original, now I would have known, beyond any argument, I had a copy and there was a better original.

Many will not like the message at first, so there is the need for love, tact and patience. Many will not want to believe that this group, which has cost them so much in time and money, is not the true one. We will be serving the Lord and fulfilling his purpose if we persist in comparing the flaws of the counterfeit with the glorious brushstrokes of the Master.

Most numerous cults

Cults in this group are probably the most numerous and the ones that you are most likely to meet. The reason is that Jehovah's Witnesses and Mormons, who regularly appear on our doorsteps, or in the local High Street, fall into this category. Most of the established cults from the nineteenth and early twentieth centuries would fall into this category.

They would bring a message about Jesus and would want to identify themselves with being 'normal' and sometimes even mainstream Christians.

How can you find out whether or not a group falls into this category? The simplest way is to take a piece of paper and on the left-hand side write down some of the important statements about Jesus from the Bible.

Some examples would be: He claimed to be God. He is the only way. He was raised from the dead. He is the unique, only-begotten Son of God.

Then on the other side of the paper you would write down the corresponding statements from the group's belief.

For Jehovah's Witnesses you might put down: He is the created son of God. He is Michael the archangel. He was only raised as a spirit creature.

For the Mormons: He is Lucifer's brother. He was created like any other man. He married several wives and had children.

When you compare the two sides of the page, you have no trouble in seeing whether the Jesus is 'another' Jesus or the true one.

Examples of organisations in this category, apart from Jehovah's Witnesses and Mormons, would be Christadelphians and Christian Scientists, and we will take a detailed look at some of these groups in later chapters.

The fact that the people bringing the message may be very sincere is not the issue. The Bible makes it clear in Galatians 1:8-9 that even if an angel were to bring the message it would not make it right. Any message disagreeing with the Word of God is wrong. This has to be the basis that we use and the only basis that is sound and fair.

In the complicated world we live in today, is it possible to meet someone from one of these groups who does have a born-again experience? This is a question we are often asked. My answer, from experience of meeting people, is yes, I believe it is possible, providing they reject the group's teaching on salvation and the work of Jesus. If someone moves away from the historical roots of the group and now accepts that Jesus died for their sins and that they could be saved, they can be our brothers and sisters. There could, however, still be differences of doctrine but these will only seriously affect our fellowship if they are on central issues. I suppose one has also to ask why they remain in a group that teaches doctrine they have had to reject to be saved?

To judge or not to judge

Some find it difficult to judge such people and prefer not to do it, but this comes from a misunderstanding of Scripture. We are not to judge in the sense of condemnatory judgement. Luke 7:37-38 puts these two matters together in the context of those whom we know are our enemies. Even in these cases we are not to write people off and say that there is no hope for them. Some definitions given by the *Concise Oxford Dictionary* for the word 'judge' are, "form an opinion about, estimate, appraise". This is what we need to do; not, as another part of the definition says, "pronounce sentence on".

I will not embark here on an in-depth study of the way to judge. What I will do is underline a few examples of what Paul wrote to Timothy in his first letter.

Almost the first words (1:3-4) were that Timothy needed to judge that certain men were teaching strange doctrines and he needed to teach them otherwise. At the end of the first chapter (1:18-20) judgement is made again that certain men had rejected the faith and were no longer to be accepted as brothers. The cornerstone of the judgement to be made (6:3) is clearly the Word of God. The way to reach out and win those who are wrong is expressed in chapter 5. Paul's closing words to Timothy (6:20-21) are as he began: he must be on his guard against those people who are false.

We are taught in Scripture to discern and judge whether or not someone coming to us has received their message from God. This is the heart of the warning in 2 John that many use as an excuse not to talk to the cults. What is being said here is that we are not to allow those with false teaching the opportunity to spread it in the church. It does not and cannot mean that we are not to talk to them at all, because that would make a nonsense of the rest of the New Testament. We should add that there are also very important warnings, such as in Matthew 7:1-5, that we need to judge ourselves on the same basis and not just point the finger at others. This is the way we are to live our lives in submission to the Lord, and any questions we raise about the teachings or lifestyle of others should be based on Scripture and expressed in an attitude of love:

> "Do not quench the Spirit; do not despise prophetic utterances. But examine everything carefully; hold fast to that which is good; abstain from every form of evil."
> 1 Thessalonians 5: 19-22.

The fact that someone says "Thus says the Lord," or "The Lord revealed this to me," does not make it automatically right. We are clearly told not to despise gifts of the Spirit such as prophecy, but we are to test them against Scripture and only accept that which is good. We must weigh up and decide whether or not what is being said is of God. It is important for our own safety that we learn to judge Scripturally but, if we are leading a fellowship, it is even more vital. The spiritual lives of many whom God has placed in our care might be in danger.

In the early 1990s we received several phone calls about a Korean children's choir which was arriving at churches just before the service and asking if they could sing. The group, the Elijah Gospel Ministry, would also ask if they could sell books afterwards. One of these books was *For Your Eternal Happiness*. Many churches allowed the group to take part without checking anything about them; only afterwards having doubts and ringing us. When we put the teaching of this group to the test of another Jesus, we found some very interesting statements regarding Jesus.

Always Being Ready!

They say that if God were to give eternal life to all who knew Jesus as God's Son the Saviour, there would be few deprived of eternal life. Knowing Jesus as Saviour is not enough; we need 'experimental knowledge' of God and Jesus.

We have become God's soul. This means 'a physical God was born' and therefore we are not people who believe in Jesus, but gods derived from God's body. God and human beings are of the same genealogy and blood. The relationship is shown by the fact that God begat a human being (Adam) and a human being (Mary) gave birth to God (Jesus).

These examples of error found in the book show the group to be preaching 'another Jesus'. The fact that it was a group of happy children made no difference to the message. Many Christians would have been exposed to this false teaching because their leaders were not prepared to judge whether or not this group came from God. Can this really be right in God's eyes?

'Christianisation'

Partly as a result of the publicity of the word 'cult' around the time of Waco, and partly just as a sign of the times, many groups have been going through a 'Christianisation' process. They want to be more acceptable and lose the tag of cult. Mormons, in the Press Releases, sent out before the new temple opened in Chorley, Lancashire, in June 1998, gave the impression that they were simply another Christian denomination. How far they have travelled from their roots, because, when they began, every other church was apostate!

Many religious cults give the same outward face to the media and the world at large. We need to scratch the surface and compare their beliefs and actions with mainstream Biblical teaching. Many cults can appear in 'fancy dress' and in 'disguise' so that you don't know at first glance who they really are.

The Worldwide Church of God have changed their Statement of Faith to be acceptable to the Evangelical

Alliance, and for every individual that has followed that change with their life we rejoice. That is the process; first we see the doctrine change, but then we are looking for the individual's life to change. In other words, 'Christianisation' is just like a Christmas tree – all the decorations are put on from the outside and they have nothing to do with the inherent life of the tree. Becoming a Christian is just like an apple tree; the fruit comes from the life within.

Jesus died spiritually

One teaching that we want to look at here under the heading of 'another Jesus' is that Jesus died spiritually, went to hell and needed to be born again. Is this true? First we quote from Kenneth Copeland, an American evangelist with a large following in many countries including Britain. Whatever the dates of the quotes below, as of writing, Copeland, to our knowledge, has not changed his belief.

> "The cross of Calvary ... is where the final redemptive work of Jesus began. When Jesus cried 'it is finished' he was not speaking about the plan of redemption. There were still three days and nights to go through before he went to the throne. ... Jesus' death on the cross was only the beginning of the complete work of redemption." – *Believer's Voice of Victory*, April 1982, p.3).

A further article that appeared in the *Believer's Voice of Victory* in September 1991 helps us to understand what is being taught. Copeland was aware that the article entitled *The Price of it All* was controversial and he comments: "There are people who've almost wanted to take me out behind the church and hang me for preaching it." He says that Jesus' death on the cross only "paid the price for the covenant" and that it was His spirit being tortured in hell by the devil and his

31

hordes that actually "paid the price for our spirits to be born again". Another statement in this article seems to go even further into heresy when he writes:

> "Now, imagine after living in that kind of glorious union with the Father, having to make yourself obedient to Satan ... and to take on his nature."

The final area we mention from this article is the way he compartmentalises the sufferings of Christ into three categories. His physical suffering paid for our body's needs; His spiritual suffering by the demons in hell paid for our spiritual rebirth; and His mental anguish paid the price for our minds to be renewed. I do not intend to give an exhaustive reply here but I believe a look at a few Scriptures is vital to show the falseness of this teaching.

Which Scripture tells us that Jesus went to hell for three days? If the answer comes back Acts 2:27, 31 and 2 Peter 2:4 you must ask the person to think again. Although these Scriptures are translated 'hell' in the King James Bible, the Greek is not *gehenna* which is the word for hell. Both verses in Acts 2 have the word *hades* which is the place of the dead waiting for judgement, not the place of punishment after judgement. 2 Peter 2:4 uses a word that is unique in Scripture, *tartarous,* which again is a place of waiting for judgement.

In all the times *gehenna* is used in Scripture, nowhere does it show that Jesus spent three days in hell. How, then, can we say that He did and still be teaching that which is consistent with Scripture?

We must also underline what Scripture says happened on the cross. Just before Jesus died physically, He placed His Spirit into His Father's, *not* the devil's hands. We should also look at the phrase 'It is finished' (John 19:30). Copeland would have us believe that all Jesus was saying was, "I've made it through stage one, my sinless life is complete." But the Greek word here, *teteleslai* has the specific meaning of 'paid in full' or 'accomplished'. It is the same word as found in the previous verse (John 19:28) where we read that Jesus then knew all things were accomplished. This is not the cry of a one-third finished job, but that of a *completed* task.

In the Bible there was no death until there was sin; sin and death go together. The reason we know that death will not stop us from having eternal life is that our sin has been dealt with. When Jesus went into death there was nothing to stop Him from rising, because death could find no sin.

Finally, we can look back to the great prophecy of the coming of Christ found in Genesis 3. Immediately after the fall, God gives the hope of the Christ coming. He says to the serpent that the Christ will bruise him in the head but all that Satan will be able to do is bruise His heel. This is a picture of Christ triumphing over Satan completely, and all that Satan can do is merely touch Him on the bottom of the foot. This is the picture of the triumph of the cross not the prophecy that Christ would be tormented in hell for three days and nights. This teaching is not consistent with Scripture and therefore is presenting 'another Jesus'.

Literal

We also need to be aware of those who literally call themselves Jesus or the Messiah. One observer in America at the time of Waco said that it was not the fact of Koresh calling himself the Messiah that worried him most. What gave greater concern were the numbers of people ringing up the TV and radio chat programmes saying that Koresh could not be the Messiah because the caller was.

Moon

Another example of being the literal Messiah is found in the teaching of the Rev. Moon and the Unification Church.

For years Moon hinted at the fact that he was the Messiah until finally in 1992 he declared it publicly.

Always Being Ready!

However, it went a little beyond that, as the report by the Unification Church's own publication shows:

> "Amidst the splendour of the magnificent Little Angels Performing Arts Centre in Seoul, Rev Sun Myung Moon announced in this speech on August 24, 1992, to a distinguished audience of current and former heads of state, scholars, professors and religious leaders, that he **and Mrs Moon** were the Lord of the Second Coming – the True Parents – the Messiah."
> – Unification *Newsletter*, Vol. 8, No. 1 (Jan 1993), p. 2, [emphasis added].

These types of declarations will not fool many Christians and the initial reaction is to laugh at them. What we must remember is that they will fool others and we need to be aware that many will come, as the Scripture says, claiming to be Jesus. We need also to be ready to show people the difference between the one making the claim of being Jesus and the real Son of God.

3 - 'Different Spirit' Cults

When we move on to the area of a different spirit, we are going to discover groups that contain people who you have no doubt are Christians; they may even teach some doctrines that are correct and encouraging. They may have areas of lifestyle that are commendable and yet there are other areas that certainly do not match up with the foundation of the Word of God. What do we do in such cases?

Some Christians, leaders among them, have said that we should do nothing. These people are serving the Lord and we must not criticise them. For reasons that we have already stated, we believe that we cannot just ignore clearly unbiblical teaching or excessive lifestyle. But neither must we be too quick to label these groups definitely as cults and to treat them as such. I am not sure that is fair when there are some good things about them. I believe that we cannot label these groups as non-Christian but we must not be afraid to offend, and call the bad, just that.

Some groups will be easier to classify than others. Some, despite having Christians within, have clear cultic tendencies. On a scale of one to ten, with ten being a fully fledged cult, they might rate seven or eight. Others would be right down at three or four and would be difficult to define. That is why, for these groups, I often use the phrase 'a Christian cult'. There will be Christians within them and they will teach some Christian principles but there will also be clear cultic tendencies. They may teach that Jesus is God, but you could also find exclusiveness in that they believe that they are the only true Church. The gospel they preach might be one of salvation by faith but there could be an authoritarian leadership. We must be clear how we define these groups but we must sound a definite warning where teachings are false.

Not a new phenomenon

Some of us might feel that we are living in unusual days, but these types of groups are not new at all. A quick look at the letters to the churches in the book of Revelation shows this. We first read about the church in Ephesus (Revelation 2:1-7) where the Lord had some strong words to say to them about leaving their first love. However, we read in verse six that the Lord commends them for one thing: that they hate the deeds of the Nicolaitans. We are not told anything about this group except that the Lord hates their deeds. Some say that they were a group who preached moral looseness, others that from their name we get the idea of lording it over the people. Interestingly, either way would describe groups that we have today. Here is the first example of a group of people within the church who, in one way or more, are not following the Lord. The Lord's verdict is that He hates their deeds.

Smyrna (Revelation 2:8-11) had dealings with groups who were probably more akin to occultic than cult groups today. Pergamum (Revelation 2:12-17), on the other hand, had their cult problem. They were not commended as in Ephesus because unfortunately they accepted these groups among them. These were people who held the teaching of Balaam. 2 Peter 2:15-16 sums up the attitude of this group: they loved the wages of unrighteousness. In the Old Testament, Balaam, knowing what the true way was, took a bribe. His heart was not devoted wholly to the Lord. In 2 Peter 2:10 we find the interesting phrase, 'those who indulge in the flesh'. This seems to sum up those who followed Balaam. Revelation adds that they also accepted some who hold the teaching of the Nicolaitans and so it would appear that the groups were similar.

The picture I get here is of people who know the way of truth and righteousness but who want to indulge the flesh, and who are prepared to take Scriptures out of context and twist them to give themselves licence for doing so. God is against those who do this, and indeed those who sit back and allow it to happen. There are groups today who fall clearly into this category. We are sometimes amazed at the fall of the American evangelists and yet here we have those who are acting in the same way. If we indulge the flesh, seeking to pamper and gratify it, we will soon find scriptures that we can take out of context to justify ourselves. Koresh is an example. 'The Family', who we will mention again later in the chapter, defend their liberal position on sex. Soon after Waco, in a live debate on Central Television, one of their leaders said that if David and Solomon had concubines there was nothing wrong with looking after the sexual needs of their unmarried members. We must be careful not to cast stones – I for one know that there but for the grace of God, go I. However, we must also be careful to warn about groups in which this sort of thing is happening today.

When we come to Thyatira (Revelation 2:18-29), we find the cult of Jezebel. Again the cult is linked with immorality but there is one other aspect that I want to underline. Jezebel called herself a prophetess. There is the true ministry of a prophet but there is also the counterfeit. The church at Thyatira tolerated Jezebel and her message, a message that encouraged people towards evil (1 Kings 21:25). Similar things are happening today; how can we know and be sure about prophets, whether or not they are of God?

There are two main tests given within Scripture: first, Deuteronomy 18:22 tells us that if what has been prophesied does not come true, we need not be afraid of that prophet. Second, 1 Peter 1:20-21 shows that the prophetic word of Scripture is not of private interpretation. It is the same today: prophecy must match up to Scripture. If the church had taken Jezebel's message and tested it, they would have seen clearly that her teaching was not from God. No matter how charismatic or famous or powerful a prophet is, we must test everything with the Word of God. If true, then we are to listen to them as prophets of God. We are to accept and take note of the command or encouragement or correction. However, each message must be tested, because some can start according to Scripture but depart from the firm foundation as popularity or other temptations arise.

In the rest of the letters to the churches, there are no other specific cults mentioned. There are two other verses, however, that mention related cultic tendencies. We read in the letter to Sardis (Revelation 3:1-6) that they had a name for being alive but were actually dead. We can sum up this thought in one word: hypocrisy. Praising God when you are feeling low is not hypocrisy. Witnessing about Jesus when you are having a tough time is not hypocrisy. The true definition of hypocrisy is pretending to be something on the outside that is not true inside. Hypocrisy is described as 'the leaven of the Pharisees' (Luke 12:1), that which can get in and adversely affect the whole. The Pharisees were concerned with outward and visible things but ignored the inward, unseen, important matters. Tombs may be beautifully painted on the outside, but they are still full of dead men's bones.

This is the theme of the letter to the church in Laodicea (Revelation 3:14-22), the church that many feel best corresponds to the days we are living in. The Lord was going to spit them out of His mouth because they made false declarations. They said that they were rich and did not need anything but actually they were poor and in terrible need. We are living in days when 'positive confession' is taught as coming from God – you only have to 'name it and claim it' and it is yours. This is the teaching prevalent today but I believe these verses show how wrong this is. It is of another spirit and not of the Spirit of God. If God moves in a miraculous way it will not be because we have pretended something has happened, it will be because He has done it. If we are poor we need to admit that we are poor and in need. Then we are to look to the Lord and give glory to Him. He can move in our lives and lead us into abundance if He wishes. However, we can also trust him in our poverty if we do not receive that abundance.

Touch not the anointed

I have already mentioned Kenneth Copeland, and there are other Christian leaders who teach the things mentioned above. I have been warned before, and some may be thinking now, that we must not touch the Lord's anointed. I do not want to put myself deliberately in a position of God's judgement and displeasure and I believe it is important to understand 1 Samuel 24:6:

> "So he said to his men, 'Far be it from me because of the Lord that I should do this thing to my lord, the Lord's anointed, to stretch out my hand against him, since he is the Lord's anointed.'"

David knew that God had anointed Saul to be king and as such he would not take his life. If God wanted Saul removed, He would have to do it Himself. This goes for anyone who has been anointed by God for a ministry; it is God's ministry and He can open the door and He can close it. We must never try to remove a person from a ministry that God has given.

Notice, however, what David did. First, he dissociated himself from Saul because he knew he was not following God any more. Second, he made it clear to those who gathered to him why he had left Saul after winning such a great victory. Third, he was still walking with God and being used by Him. I believe the lesson is there for us today. In the right spirit and in the right way we can point out the Biblical errors of people who are well known and often well accepted. It is not wrong to disassociate ourselves from them and that does not mean that God will not use us. It is vital that we are aware of the different spirit that is prevalent in the church today.

This chapter will end with some examples. I am not implying that those I am going to mention are not Christians and I would not want to suggest that everything they say is wrong or of no value. If I said that I would be lying. What I *am* saying is that in some areas I believe they have departed from the truth and we need to accept that and take whatever action is necessary.

If an adult is presented with a mixture of good and bad fruit they can probably pick their way through it and discard those that would be harmful. Young children would not have the same capability and would probably eat the rotten fruit. The same is true in the Christian faith. Mature believers who have a grounding in the Word of God could probably discern. Young Christians will not have the same ability, but will work on the assumption that if people are right in one thing they are right in all; and there is the danger. I am not starting a hate so-and-so campaign, but I do believe we need to wake up to ways in which a different spirit may be creeping into the church.

I will start with the correspondence I have had with the Kenneth Copeland office concerning his beliefs, and indeed the beliefs of others in the Word of Faith Movement. Not every word they say is wrong but I want to underline just a couple of areas that give me great concern. The first we have already touched upon: proclaiming something is true in your life when it is not. In an article in one of Reachout's newsletters we quoted from one of Copeland's books,

> "Adam was created in God's class ... to rule as a god .., by speaking words."

Kenneth Copeland Ministries responded to this as follows:

> "The full title of the publication from which the quotation in this section was taken is *The Power of the Tongue* by Kenneth Copeland. In Genesis 1:1 (and Hebrews 11:3), we read that God created the heavens and earth by the power of the spoken word, and that he delegated this power to man he created (Genesis 1:28: 2:19, 20). Mark 11:23 underlines the importance of faith-filled words and James chapter 3 advises us of the power of words, both positive and negative. The teaching of the truth concerning our use of words must be seen in the context of our submission to God's authority in our lives, so

> that we do not fall into the trap of wanting to
> grab all that we can for ourselves, whether
> this is power, influence, material possessions
> or anything else."

From this last sentence we must surely draw the conclusion that Copeland Ministries believe it is possible to obtain power, influence and material possessions by the proclamation of a word. It is, they believe, possible to 'get what you say'. Is this Biblical?

They rightly say that God created through the power of the Word. Only God can speak and it is done. However, the verses quoted in Genesis do not show Adam creating *anything* by his word. Genesis 1:28 tells Adam to subdue the earth, but does not say it is by the word. Genesis 2:19-20 shows God creating and Adam naming the animals. Neither of these verses has anything to do with speaking out a word and it coming to pass. Is there anywhere in the Scriptures that tell us that God has passed on this ability? No. The nearest is, of course, the prophetic word that comes direct from God, and we know it is direct from God because it comes to pass. As far as we can see from Scripture, then, the only one who can make something happen simply by His word is God.

I agree that we must be careful what we say and how we say it. Our words can hurt people. If I continually tell my children how hopeless they are, then they are likely to receive emotional damage and feel they are hopeless. However, if I simply say, 'I think it's going to be a bad day', that will not happen because of saying it. Believing that is no better than believing that breaking a mirror will bring seven years' bad luck: both are superstition.

What about the other scriptures mentioned in the response quoted? In Mark 11:23 the mountain will only move if God has told me to proclaim it. Proclaiming those words without the faith that has come from God will produce nothing, no matter how much I try to work it up. What about James 3? James does indeed teach us that we must be careful what we say, but in the context of starting a flame of bitterness or hatred or suchlike. Nowhere does James teach us that we must be careful what we say because what we say is what we are going to get.

If I start proclaiming things simply because I want them to be true, then I will start living the hypocritical life. We read in Romans 4 that Abraham knew he and Sarah were past the age for bearing children but he did not just ignore that and proclaim the opposite. He looked directly at the problem, admitted exactly what it was and then looked at God and gave Him the glory. This is very different from the teaching of proclaiming words. We believe that this can be a dangerous teaching – several people have got themselves into spiritual trouble using this formula.

I believe there is also one other teaching of the Word Faith Movement that needs to be mentioned here, the so-called 'prosperity doctrine'.

This teaching is divisive as it misses the point: that some Christians will live in poverty all their lives. It also misses out the truth that to gain our life we must lose it. Prosperity teaching is fine for the few who live in expensive houses, but it is not like that for most people. Maybe God's prosperity is the raven bringing a few crumbs of food or the one meal of corn bread a day that Elijah knew.

Kenneth Copeland Ministries said in their response to me:

> "...a large proportion of the world's wealth is in the hands of very few people, many of whom have gained it by unscrupulous means. It is in the Church's power to get hold of this wealth in order to distribute it to those in need, because the root behind this injustice is sin. As we get hold of God's principles for financial prosperity, then the Church will be able to go ahead with the task that so desperately needs doing. It is happening in some instances, but all the time we resist the truth that it is God's will to prosper us, we shall not get very far."

If it is God's will to prosper me, then, as with any other aspect of my Christian life, I believe His words, receive them by faith and wait expectantly for Him to bring it to pass. I know of no Scripture that tells us that the church needs the world's wealth. Jesus taught that we are to give to Caesar what belongs to him; not take it away even if it was received unscrupulously. We may be aware of financial need in these days, but the early church did not find the lack of finance a hindrance to preaching the gospel.

Please consider carefully if the following Copeland statement is Scriptural:

> "You give $1 for the Gospel's sake and $100 belongs to you; you give $10 and you receive $1000: give $1000 and receive $10,000. I know that you can multiply, but I want you to see it in black and white ... Give one airplane and receive one hundred times the value of the airplane. Give one car and the return would furnish you a lifetime of cars. In short Mark 10:30 is a very good deal."

If we followed that through logically, then every giving Christian, and there are thousands of them, would be a millionaire in a year. This is not what happens, though. Are we then to say to those who are not wealthy that it is because of lack of faith? If I believe the above, I would have to say simply that God did not keep His part of the bargain!

Mark 10:30, in the quotation above, is used by Copeland Ministries in the context of money and possessions but the Scripture puts it in terms of family and livelihood. The quotation puts it in the context of what has been given; the Scripture puts it in the context of what has been left behind. The giving of money and possessions is not even mentioned and therefore we have no right to expect this to be honoured by the Lord. As far as the apostles were concerned they left their families behind, but God loved them and protected them. They left their means of livelihood behind but God provided what was needed for them. These verses say that what we give up for the sake of preaching the gospel, God will make up to us a hundredfold. However, we should also expect to receive persecutions. This is the promise that God will honour and no more.

Prosperity teaching is of a different spirit and if we want to accept it we must be aware that we are accepting a teaching not backed up by Scripture.

I hope a look at these two elements of the Word of Faith Movement will also help us to assess other doctrines according to the Biblical foundation.

Benny Hinn

Benny Hinn is a very popular preacher and many are horrified that we would put him in this section. However, I relate several facts concerning him below, which can be checked out and verified. If these things are not in line with mainstream Christianity and he is guilty of false teaching and prophecy, then we do have a right to put the label 'Christian cult' over such a ministry.

Hinn claims to be under the anointing from God and so is saying, God said and did this. That is the problem. If he was just saying this is what I think or what I feel, we may not agree but it would be his opinion. However, Hinn teaches that much of what he says - and indeed all that he says under the 'anointing' - is what God says, not what he says. This is therefore serious and needs to be checked out.

Indeed, as Christians, we do not have an option as to whether we want to check it out or not; the Bible is clear what we have to do:

> "Therefore encourage one another and build up one another, just as you also are doing. But we request of you, brethren, that you appreciate those who diligently labour among you, and have charge over you in the Lord and give you instruction, and that you esteem

them very highly in love because of their work. Live in peace with one another. We urge you, brethren, admonish the unruly, encourage the fainthearted, help the weak, be patient with all men. See that no one repays another with evil for evil, but always seek after that which is good for one another and for all men. Rejoice always; pray without ceasing; in everything give thanks; for this is God's will for you in Christ Jesus. Do not quench the Spirit; do not despise prophetic utterances. But examine everything carefully; hold fast to that which is good." - 1 Thessalonians 5:11-21

Here we have it. Yes, we are to encourage one another, and we are to appreciate those that work for the Lord in our midst. However, at the same time, we are to admonish and above all, "examine everything carefully". This is especially mentioned in the light of prophetic utterances. The outcome is that we are then to hold fast to that which is good - having left behind that which is not good!

Where there are prophetic utterances - those words that are said to come from the Holy Spirit - we need to examine them in detail. Whatever your feelings are concerning Benny Hinn, what are your feelings about God's Word? Can someone who has given such clear false prophecies - see just two examples below - in the name of the Lord really be part of the 'good' that we are to hold on to?

"The Spirit tells me - Fidel Castro will die - in the 90's. Oooh my! Some will try to kill him and they will not succeed. But there will come a change in his physical health, and he will not stay in power, and Cuba will be visited of God." - Orlando Christian Centre, 31 December 1989.

"The Lord also tells me to tell you in the mid 90's, about '94-'95, no later than that, God will

> destroy the homosexual community of America. But He will not destroy it - with what many minds have thought Him to be, He will destroy it with fire. And many will turn and be saved, and many will rebel and be destroyed." - Orlando Christian Centre, 31 December 1989.

Not only is it direct prophecy that is a problem, but some of the messages he gives and actions he takes. Below is the transcript of part of the video of a meeting in Denver, Colorado, on 17 September 1999. Please will you test it out - are these words really coming from God, as Hinn claims? If not, then this is a serious case of fraud:

> "...I place a curse on every man and every woman that would stretch his hand against this anointing, I curse that man who dares to speak a word against this ministry and any man and any woman that raises his or her hand in blessing towards this ministry I bless that man, I bless that home, I bless that family. Any man, any woman, any person that raises his tongue in blessings towards this work, raises his tongue in blessing towards this anointing, raises his tongue in blessing towards this servant of the Lord, I bless them. I bless the work the work of your hand, I bless your life with this mighty power. I bless your home with the divine protection, I bless your children with long life and I bless you with length of days, I bless you with health and healing, I bless with prosperity, I bless you with the very presence of Almighty God, I a servant bless you. In the name of the one I serve, I bless thy people the night in Denver.
>
> "Lift your hands and receive the blessing people, I rarely ever do what I am doing now, this is the Holy Ghost on me telling me to do

this. I bless you; I bless your homes, your life, your future, your children. May every attack of Satan against you be destroyed, may every plan of hell be destroyed against you and every plan of God be established, in Jesus name. Amen. Amen.

"Under this anointing, under this anointing the word I speak cannot fall to the ground, under this anointing every thing I say happens."

Please note these last words carefully. This means that everyone who questions Benny Hinn and his ministry is cursed. Everyone that checks out his teaching and shows that is not according to mainstream Christian teaching is cursed. Yet this is the opposite of what the Scripture says, "examine everything carefully" and only hold fast that which is good. Who are we to believe: the Scripture or the 'anointed' utterance of Benny Hinn? Choosing both is not an option there.

We could continue with looking at his teaching that differs from mainstream Christianity, but I believe there is enough to see why we put such men as this in this category and why we need to be very carefully in checking out all teaching and prophecy, whoever gives it.

The Family

The 1970s saw the rise of the Children of God. Hounded from country to country, their leader David 'Moses' Berg wrote several pornographic pamphlets. One of his milder instructions was that children should be encouraged to indulge in nude mixed bathing, experimentation, play, etc., but not in front of visitors. Today the group has changed its image and is called The Family.

They claim, on their website, to have approximately 12,000 full-time and associate adult volunteer members working out of over 1,400 centres, situated in over 100 countries. I am sure there are many Christians within this number, especially with their teaching of initial salvation being by grace, but they do hold very liberal views on sex between consenting adults.

Nowhere, to my knowledge, has there been true repentance, simply a change of name. Where are those who have come forward, and not just said they have changed, but have confessed they were wrong in the past? Where are those who have given themselves up to the courts to decide the matter?

Their website has this paragraph:

> "In 1976, David proposed an unprecedented corollary to the Law of Love: He contended that, in certain circumstances, it would be acceptable for a Christian to have sexual relations with someone in an effort to demonstrate a tangible manifestation of God's Love, thereby helping them to come to a saving knowledge of Jesus Christ. This doctrine became known as "Flirty Fishing," a term that David adapted from Jesus' admonition to His disciples to 'follow Me, and I will make you fishers of men' (Matthew 4:19). It was practiced by many Family members until 1987, when it was discontinued, largely due to the need to spend more time in other forms of outreach."

Notice why it was discontinued: not because it was wrong, but they wanted to spend time in other forms of outreach. In email exchanges it has been noted that indeed they still defend the practice, not confess it as wrong.

The Bible shows in James (3:11-12) that sweet and bitter waters cannot come from the same source. David Berg, who died in 1994, could write inspiring articles up until his death, about obedience, faith, love, etc., but this does not make up for the ones he wrote encouraging incest in the past.

Until there is true Biblical repentance and past teaching fully cleared up, I will always have doubts about this group. A change in name and style is not enough; we need to see evidence of a distinct change of the heart.

There are also areas of concern in their teaching. For instance, in their dealing with spirits and the occult realm there may be some danger that members will open themselves up to evil spirits. They teach that sometimes the spiritual messengers sent in the Bible were not angels but the spirits of some former people of God. What makes this even worse is that they go on to teach that this is still happening today:

> "We believe that in addition to angelic ministering spirits, God on occasion also uses the spirits of departed saints to minister and deliver messages to His people." – TheFamily.org Website

This group, who announce themselves as evangelical Christians, are teaching occultic practices along with mainstream Christian teaching.

International Churches of Christ

Another example of this 'different spirit' is the Boston Church Movement or, as it is officially known today, the International Churches of Christ. This group was a breakaway from the denomination of the Church of Christ who has often disowned them.

There are Christians within this group, but it also shows some classic cultic tendencies. They believe that an individual *must* be baptised to be saved. However, it is more than that; you must be baptised into *their church*. Whether you have believed in Christ before, whether you have repented from your sins, or even whether you have been baptised as confession of your faith is irrelevant. The only way to salvation is through joining their church.

See chapter 15 on p.199 for a detailed look at this group.

4 - 'Different Gospel' Cults

Paul starts his letter to the Galatians (1:6-9) with amazement that the Christians could accept another gospel that was really not a gospel. Paul emphasises that the only basis for the gospel is Jesus Christ alone. The moment we seek to add to the grace of God we are not on the true foundation of Christ.

Salvation by works

A verse from the *Book of Mormon* sums up the teaching of the Church of Jesus Christ of the Latter-day Saints very well,

> "For we labor diligently to write, to persuade our children, and also our brethren, to believe in Christ, and to be reconciled to God; for we know that it is by grace that we are saved, after all we can do." - 2 Nephi 25:23

Yes, the grace of God will kick in at some point, but first we must be working hard at it.

Many established cults such as Mormons and Jehovah's Witnesses would also be described by this heading.

As with the cults of another Jesus, these are easy to spot. Take a blank piece of paper and on the left-hand side write down several key factors about the gospel. There would be such headings as, only by grace; through faith in Jesus Christ; the penalty of my sin taken by Jesus, and so on. Then on the right-hand side write down what a particular group believes. The moment you find a statement that shows that works are essential for salvation, or that you need to belong to a particular organisation to be saved, then you know that you have a different gospel.

We should notice too that Paul talks in Galatians (1:6) about those who quickly desert the gospel. We will find many people in the cults who have had some brush with church or Christianity in the past but for some reason it did not satisfy. They have now moved away into a different gospel.

Always Being Ready!

Another phrase that is very relevant to the cults is 'not straightforward about the truth' (2:14). The truth is taken and twisted like a corkscrew. Outward signs that are not important are once again held in high esteem. In the Gentile world we may not have a problem with circumcision, but there are many groups that will tell us that the outward sign of baptism is essential to salvation. This is such an important matter that a section of chapter 10 will be devoted to it.

Brotherhood of Cross & Star

This is an example of a group that has more recently established itself in Britain, although its roots go back to the 16th century, when a Biakpan tribal prophetess called Otom had the first pre-birth appearance of Olumba Olumba Obu, the founder of the Brotherhood of the Cross and Star movement.

Their gospel becomes one of works, and especially obedience to O.O.Obu:

> "The words of God in BCS are the most powerful weapon, as it comes directly from the author of words and wisdom and is based solely on 'love one another'. It is the truth enriched with love, comfort, strength, faith, contentment, assurance, hope and revelations. The Gospels from the Sole spiritual Head of the Universe is the only path to purification, righteousness and salvation." – http://freespace.virgin.net/dolly.daniels/ WHAT_IS_BCS.HTML

A full investigation into their teachings can be found on our website at http://www.reachouttrust.org/regulars/articles/cult/ bhdstar.htm. This article concludes as follows:

> "The distinct impression which a study of this movement gives is that O.O.Obu who was not well taught in Bible truth made what he could

of sound doctrine and became increasingly adrift as the years went on. This was compounded by occult activity. The main factor which seems to have led the movement becoming another religion is making the mistake of teaching the Bible without any reference to sound hermeneutics. Does that sound familiar? The fact is, as any marksman knows, the aim only needs to be ever so slightly off centre to miss the target completely."

Paul C Jong

Many will not have heard of this South Korean preacher, but his teaching found on various websites is indeed a 'different' gospel.

The basic belief breaks down in to three areas. First, John the Baptist is like the High Priest and passed all the sins of mankind on to Jesus. Second, we are cleansed from sin once and for all through, first, the gospel of water (baptism). If we do not believe correctly about Jesus then it is impossible to be saved. And third, baptism has special spiritual meaning of passing on sin by laying on of hands.

However, nowhere does the Bible speak of John as a High Priest - even though from the family of priests (Luke 1). John is always spoken of in terms of being a forerunner, looking forward to someone else. There is also not one Scripture that talks about John placing the sin of mankind on Jesus, indeed it is said that the Lord did it (Isaiah 53:6).

Emphasis is put on correct understanding in order for your sins to be forgiven. This means that some can never be saved because some will not just understand. Jong claims that if you do not know the truth then you commit the sin of disobedience. This is illogical because, if you do not know something, you are not disobeying.

However, the central area we must look at is baptism as this becomes the key for the forgiveness of my sin, and without an understanding of what Jong says happens, then I cannot have my sin forgiven and I am on my way to hell.

But not one Scripture talks of sin being passed on to Jesus by John. Indeed, evidence surrounding the event would suggest otherwise. First, John wanted to prevent Jesus from being baptized (Matthew 3:14) - that would not have happened if he knew the vital act that was about to take place. And second, when Jesus was baptized, heaven was opened (Luke 3:21, 22). The opposite reaction as to when Jesus dies on the Cross – the Father turns away and we have darkness.

Hebrews 9:13-16 shows that, for there to be forgiveness of sin, there needs to be the sacrifice and blood being shed. Neither of these things happened at Baptism, only at Calvary.

1 Peter 3:21 is often used by those seeking to prove that baptism is necessary for salvation. At first glance, it may appear that this Scripture teaches that baptism now saves you, but note in the previous verses to what it is corresponding. Baptism saving you corresponds to the flood. We need to discover three things here. What actually saved the people from the flood; what was the salvation from; and what was it to.

If this was to teach us that New Testament baptism saves, then we would need to see that it was the water that saved Noah and his family. However, the water did not save them; rather the opposite – it nearly destroyed them. What actually saved them was the ark. We need to discover in New Testament terms what or whom the Old Testament picture of the ark represents, and the answer is not baptism but Jesus Christ. Being put into water does not save us; our safety comes from being in Christ and having a sure relationship with Him.

What sort of salvation was this? Are we talking about the salvation of receiving Christ into the life? No, in Old Testament terms, they needed that relationship before they got into the ark. This was a salvation that would take them out of one world system into another. Salvation is not being used here in the sense of being born again. It is a full deliverance, through God's judgment, into the new world order that Christ has yet to set up on earth

The conclusion we reach on Jong's gospel is that it is not seen within Scripture, and should be rejected by all those who want to embrace the truth of mainstream Christianity.

Secret knowledge

Paul dealt with this area when he wrote to the Colossians. The Gnostic 'gospel' is that you need the special or secret knowledge that can only come from our group. Jesus Christ is not enough; there are extra or mystical revelations that need to be added. Paul cuts the ground away from these groups by stating (2:3) that all the treasures of wisdom and knowledge are in Christ. Again (2:8-9) he shows that all the fullness of God is in Christ and we do not need to add any vain traditions of man.

There are several groups that would come under this heading of providing secret knowledge. One illustration that most people would be aware of is the Freemasons. Freemasonry is very secretive.

Freemasonry

> "Masonry, like all the religions... conceals its secrets from all except the adepts and sages or the elect and uses *false* explanations and misinterpretations of its symbols to mislead those who deserve only to be misled; to conceal the truth which it calls *light...*" – A. Pike, *Morals and Dogma of the Ancient and Accepted Scottish Rite of Freemasonry*, pp. 104–105.

Freemasonry extends its influence through government, administrations of justice, professional bodies, all levels of management, local authorities and, sadly, the church. Some members of the Royal Family have been connected with Masonic ritual. The Duke of Kent holds the title of Grand Master.

Always Being Ready!

When confronted with some facts, Masons will say you are totally wrong. However, remember it is a secret society and only as you progress do you find out more. In common with many cults, a Mason will only listen to a masonic teacher and would regard all that he reads in books, etc., as wrong.

There are the funny handshakes and the initiation ceremonies; the ways of standing and the sayings that identify Masons to each other the world over. There is also some influence from the occult and there is help given to Masons by fellow Masons in business. In some cases, it is even claimed that judges have given lighter sentences to known Masons.

You cannot apply to join but must be invited by someone already in the society. Still, there are over 3,000,000 Masons worldwide with possibly up to a third of these in the 7,500 British lodges.

In Britain most Masons go no higher than the third degree, called Master Mason. In Scottish Rite Masonry this is the third of a possible thirty-three degrees. The system of advancement through the degrees is complex, with each order and level having its own passwords and secrets not known to the lower degrees. This causes the ignorance and deception of the initiates.

> "The Blue Degrees... (Craft Masons) ... are intentionally misled by false interpretations. **It is not intended that he shall understand them but it is intended that he shall imagine he understands them.**" – A. Pike, *Morals and Dogma of the Ancient and Accepted Scottish Rite of Freemasonry*, Reprinted 1966. (Emphasis added.)

Oaths were added to Masonry some time during the eighteenth century. Today the new candidate needs to go through the initiation ceremony of the 'entered apprentice'. He is blindfolded, a noose placed about his neck, his left breast bared and one trouser leg rolled up. Then he is brought into the Lodge, where a dagger is placed to his chest. He later commits himself to the oath:

> "... binding myself under no less penalty than that of having my throat cut across, my tongue torn out by its roots and my body buried in the rough sands of the sea at low water mark."

The Fellow Craft degree follows a similar pattern and the Master Mason puts himself:

> "... under no less a penalty than that of having my body severed in two, my bowels taken from thence and burned to ashes, the ashes being scattered before the four winds of heaven..."

The Master Mason also swears to keep a brother's secrets "... murder and treason excepted", but in the later Royal Arch degree murder and treason are not excepted. Thus, at least in words, the Masonic oath is placed above the law and country. These oaths are taken on the Volume of the Sacred Law (VOSL) which in Britain is normally a Bible. However, in respective countries it can equally be the Talmud, Koran or any Hindu or other religious writings.

All roads lead to God

Nothing has done more to water down the gospel than the belief that all roads lead to God. It is unpopular to say that there is only one way to the true God, but that is the revelation from Scripture.

Bahá'i

Members of the Bahá'i belief system would come into this group; they accept that there are merits in all world religions but all must accede to the supremacy of God's revelation to Bahá'u'lláh. Jesus is only one of nine manifestations of God , although all major religions hold some truth, it is not worked out in practice. The belief of a Bahá'i can be summed up in three statements:

Oneness of God – God is one and there is but one God for all the world. He is the Creator, Infinite and All-knowing. He is known to humanity only through his messengers.

Oneness of all religions – All the great religions come originally from God, revealed through his messengers. They are fulfilled in the Bahá'i faith.

Oneness of mankind – All belong to the same human family. Bahá'u'lláh says, "The earth is but one country and mankind its citizens."

Groups who believe that all roads lead to the same God are becoming more numerous. With such belief it does not matter which path we take and it becomes very comfortable. Many New Age cults fit firmly in this section and their influence is extending into the church itself.

Do all roads lead to God? Simply, the answer is yes ... and no. The roads that these groups are taking lead to god with a small 'g', to a supernatural power that is an impostor and a deceiver. They do not lead to the creator God of the Scriptures. Some would call us racist for saying the Hindu path or the Buddhist path does not lead to God, but it is not being racist, it is being logical. Ask the Hindu for his definition of God and he will talk about an invisible force. As you listen to his definition you will see how different it is from the definition of the God of Scripture. Hindus admit themselves that they are travelling to a different god. The god they worship is different from the One we worship; we simply agree with them. We were told by one Christian visiting our stand at Spring Harvest that because it's a free country we should not try to change anyone's religion. How tragic: that would mean that thousands would never have the chance to hear the real gospel and find the one true road.

New Age cults

The common beliefs of the New Age Movement lead to a gospel that is the opposite of the Christian gospel. They accept *monism* – all is one and everything that exists is interrelated. This, however, strikes at the heart of Christian belief because the Bible shows that there is a clear distinction between the Creator and His creation. From here the New Ager moves on to *pantheism* – all is 'god' or at least god is in everything. Everything is an expression of god and therefore we too are gods.

The outcome of these beliefs is a different gospel; Jesus Christ is not unique and we do not need salvation in a God outside us because we are god, or at least we contain god already. We must achieve the reality of releasing the 'god-force' within ourselves.

As all roads lead up the mountain, I can take whichever path seems good to me to achieve my objective. I must not criticise the path others take nor do I expect criticism about the way I go. The gospel of the New Age Movement and Christianity are poles apart. The New Ager says you can do it; think positively and you'll get it. God says you can never do it by yourself; give up and let Me do it in you. Consider yourself dead and let me live within you. (Galatians 2:20).

Reincarnation

The difference between New Age belief and Christianity can especially be seen when a comparison is made between reincarnation – the means by which the New Ager hopes to reach their goal – and resurrection, the hope of the Christian.

Many people that we talk to today have a worldview that embraces reincarnation rather than resurrection. It is, therefore, necessary for us both to understand what we are talking about and know how to communicate sensibly with someone who has that worldview.

Always Being Ready!

We can first question the whole basis of reincarnation. It may not be as comforting to those who believe if the facts are communicated clearly to them. There are a number of questions and suggestions you can bring to these folks even if they do not believe in God and the Bible.

For instance, at the end of life number one, you will have committed more bad than good. The accounts will not balance and you will not be able to be released from the body into your 'eternal inheritance'. You have what could be called your 'karmic debt'. Later you start life number two with your original karmic debt. Try as you might you still do more bad than good, and so what happens at the end of this life? A bigger karmic debt!

Reincarnation is not an easy payment plan; it is a hard taskmaster. You will never be able to balance the accounts no matter how many lives you live. There is no hope - just an endless round of lives going nowhere.

Once you have got to that point of showing just how hopeless the position is you can ask them, "How would you feel if someone came along and offered to pay off all your debts when you next die?" How different they would feel about life; what certainty they would have; how they would begin to look forward to the future life knowing what was to come instead of simply hoping that this may be the one!

You have, of course, introduced the concept of redemption without at first mentioning sin or the cross, etc. You can then, through your testimony, show that this is what has happened to you and from these you can also show that this is the Bible message. How much more certain than the 'hope' of reincarnation.

There are those who believe that reincarnation is taught in Scripture and try to harmonise reincarnation and the Bible. The basis of belief in reincarnation does away with eternal punishment. However, the Bible clearly teaches that although God wishes none to perish some will refuse the saving grace He offers. [2 Peter 3:9; Revelation 20:13-15]

'Different Gospel' Cults

The Bible shows that the only hope of salvation is to trust in the finished and completed work of Jesus Christ. Reincarnation feels it must add to this several hundred or thousand lifetimes full of striving. [John 14:6; Acts 4:10-12]

The Bible states that there is one life, one death, and then we stand before the judgement seat of Christ. Reincarnation talks about multiple lives and deaths and no once-and-for-all judgement. [Hebrews 9:27]

The Bible teaches the marvellous doctrine of justification - God pronouncing us righteous and treating us accordingly. Reincarnation gives no hope of justification; we will never be in such an intimate relationship with the living God. [Romans 5:1]

One of the key themes of scripture is the peace of knowing our sins forgiven. Reincarnation only ever offers the potential of counteracting the negative Karma with the positive Karma. Sin is never actually dealt with and so there can be no dealing with the guilt of the past. [1 John 1:8-9]

Grace, similarly, is neglected by reincarnation because we only receive what we 'deserve'. God would never 'lower' Himself to pick us up and give us that which we do not deserve. The Bible, however, spells out the abundant grace of God again and again. [2 Corinthians 8:9]

In summary, we would have to say that the central theme of the Bible is that the Love of God wants to deal with the root problem (sin) in our lives so that we can know a life of contentment in the Lord. Reincarnation, on the other hand, will often do just the opposite because of the fear of upsetting the positive Karma the person might be receiving by suffering.

5 - Secular Cults

All the cults that we have mentioned so far have something in common. They lead their members to some form of 'spiritual' life. There are cults, though, that do not use the person of Jesus, except maybe as an historic figure, or base their teachings on religious writings. For the purposes of this book I have called them secular cults.

I will not dwell too much on them but it is good to be aware they exist. Often the approach made to these people has to be different. With those who have joined a cult for some 'spiritual' reason, at least we have common ground to use to communicate with them the true spiritual message. With secular cults, self-improvement cults, or cults simply built around someone's ideas, this common ground is rarely there.

Former Moonie Steven Hassan has written an excellent secular book, *Combatting Cult Mind Control*. Drawing on his experience and understanding, he gives insight into the mind-set of the cultist. In the book he divides cults into four main groups: religious, political, psychotherapy/educational and commercial.

From his secular viewpoint, religious cults would be the ones we have been describing so far. He does not distinguish between those that use the Bible, eastern religions or the occult.

Political cults are described by Hassan as those organised around a particular dogma. The cults which have arisen around Nazism and right-wing extremism probably fall into this category and we will need to be vigilant concerning groups like this in the future.

Psychotherapy/educational cults are the ones that hold high-priced seminars to bring 'enlightenment'. These we would mostly describe as New Age cults, such as Silva Mind Control, Est or latterly Forum, Course of Miracles and similar organisations.

Always Being Ready!

The final grouping Hassan mentions is the commercial cults and they have as their main aim the making of money. Hassan says concerning these groups:

> "They deceive and manipulate people to work for little or no pay in the hope of getting rich. There are many pyramid-style or multilevel marketing organizations that promise big money but fleece their victims. They then destroy their victims' self-esteem so that they will not complain. Success depends on recruiting new people who in turn recruit others. Other commercial cults include those that browbeat people into hawking magazine subscriptions or other items door to door. These cults take out ads in local newspapers promising exciting travel and lucrative careers. Cult recruiters set up 'interviews' inside their hotel rooms, preying on high school and college students." - Steven Hassan, *Combatting Cult Mind Control*, p.40.

Whereas Hassan is describing the American scene, he uses some descriptions that remind me of groups we are regularly asked about in this country. Although these groups are not the prime concern of Reachout Trust, we must be aware that they exist. We also need to be watchful of groups that come close to the description Hassan gives of commercial cults.

Amway, which is one of the groups that we are regularly asked about is certainly not the worst offender - details of our full investigation can be found on our website (http://www.reachouttrust.org/regulars/articles/other/amway. htm) but here we repeat our conclusions:

> "We do not feel it is our place in conclusion to tell you whether to join Amway or not. As an evangelical Christian we suggest that you take the above facts (detailed in the article)

and seek the Lord as to whether it would be helpful to your Christian life or not. We realise that this may mean that some would join and some not but that would not be a contradiction. What is God's way for one man is not necessarily His way for the next. What each one of us must be sure of is that we are living our lives according to the Word of God. We should not continually allow things, in either our attitude or actions, that knowingly contradicts the will of God for our lives as revealed in the Scripture."

Only half way

There are many, such as Steven Hassan, who are doing excellent work in the secular field and I believe that we can learn much from them, although, I feel very strongly that if we simply deprogramme a person, only half the job is done. All we will have done is bring them back to the place they started from, and they will still be vulnerable. The reason people join cults, of whatever type, is that they have a need in their life. At the point they join the cult they feel that this is the group to meet that need. This, of course, is not true, as the only One Who can really meet that need is Jesus Christ.

We must help these people to cope mentally with the trauma of what they have been through. Emotions may be shattered and they might need expert help to be able to cope with life again. Beyond all this, though, the person has a deep spiritual need. We must find ways to communicate the gospel in words that they will understand and in a way that is relevant to them. We must never force people to become Christians nor must we make it a prerequisite of helping them. What we must do is give them the opportunity to have the needs in their life met.

When Paul went to Athens, he was not just concerned with delivering the people from their 'unknown god'; he wanted them to come to know Jesus Christ. This was true for every place that he and all the apostles visited. Our aim must be to treat people in the same way today. Suppose we are successful in helping them escape a cult in this life. They may be set free but one day they will die. We have given them an existence in this life but still not shown them the way to eternal life. We must be tactful. We must show love and understanding. But, above all, our desire must be to help these people for eternity and not just for time.

Scientology

In some ways Scientology overlaps being either a secular or religious cult. Whereas they say they have no 'theology of God' and it is up to each individual to have their own views, they do in these days, for a variety of reasons, want to be seen to be religious.

For most people, their first experience of Scientology is an invitation to one of their centres to take a 'Personal Efficiency' test. The invitation might be received personally as you walk down Tottenham Court Road or a street in your town. On the other hand you might receive the 'Oxford Analysis Test', an in-depth questionnaire posted through your letterbox. Either way your character is assessed and then you will be offered courses to correct the deficiencies in your character that the tests have shown up. Accepting the invitation could mean writing cheques for hundreds of pounds over the next months. What real benefit you receive in return is certainly open to question.

At the end of 1993, Scientology headquarters in America won a long battle with the United States Internal Revenue Service. Now that they are accepted as a *bona fide* religion, and they are an official tax-exempt body, Scientologists have made much of this official recognition and are painting a very rosy picture of their organisation. Many outsiders would disagree, including some who were once part of the organisation. *The Sunday Times* (3 April 1994), contained an interesting article that described the harassment ex-Scientologists face:

"Police are investigating complaints that private investigators employed by the Church of Scientology ... have intimidated witnesses and plaintiffs in forthcoming court cases ... during six days of demonstrations outside the house of one witness, Jon Atack. Atack, a former scientologist, has devoted the last 10 years to helping victims of the cult ... (he) claims that at least 80 scientologists have committed suicide ... (and said) 'I am frankly in fear of my life and I am frightened for my children ... this has ruined my health and left me with very little money for 10 years now, but I am determined I will fight them to the death'."

The article also mentioned this quotation made in 1984:

"Scientology is both immoral and socially obnoxious. Mr Kennedy did not exaggerate when he termed it 'pernicious'. In my judgement it is corrupt, sinister and dangerous. It is corrupt because it is based on lies and deceit and has as its real objective money and power for Mr Hubbard, his wife and those close to him at the top. It is sinister because it indulges in infamous practices both against its adherents who do not toe the line unquestioningly and against those outside who criticise or oppose it. It is dangerous because it is out to capture people, especially children and impressionable young people, and indoctrinate and brainwash them so that they become the unquestioning captives and tools of the cult, withdrawn from ordinary thought, living and relationships with others."

These words were not spoken by an embittered ex-member of Scientology but by Mr Justice Latey, at the Royal Courts of Justice on 23 July, 1984.

Always Being Ready!

Active Scientologists would not, of course, agree with this definition, but it is very interesting that, as Justice Latey says, "(the) case is based largely on Scientology's own documents and as the father's counsel, Mr Johnson, candidly, albeit plaintively, said: 'What can we do to refute what is stated in Scientology's own documents?'"

In June 1999, a couple in Britain, Bonnie and Richard Woods, who run 'Escape', an organisation set up to help people wanting to leave Scientology, won an important legal battle. In it (Case 1993 W. No. 2079, High Court of Justice, Queen's Bench Division) counsel on behalf of Scientology apologised.

They acknowledge that the allegations made by them about Mrs Woods were untrue and apologised. They also agreed to pay Mrs Woods a substantial amount of money in respect of her claim and undertook no longer to make these untrue accusations against her.

Defendant's Counsel said,

> "On behalf of the Church of Scientology and all the Defendants I wish to associate myself with all that has been said by counsel for the Plaintiff. The Defendants regret that when responding to Mrs Woods' criticisms of the Church of Scientology they went too far in attributing to her conduct and motives which they now accept were not correct. Through me they apologise to Mrs Woods and undertake (in the terms of the draft Order before Your Lordship) not to make any such allegations again."

Actions and attitudes of Scientologists towards its 'enemies' does seem to have softened of late and there are few if any reports of harassment of former members.

However, if they *are* a secular cult, what are the teachings of the Scientologist that attract people to join in the first place? In essence, Scientology seeks to bring individuals to a sufficient understanding of themselves and show them how they can improve their ways. Scientologists leave out God, church and the Bible from their definition but they are still seeking to change people for the better. Scientology is a do-it-yourself answer. We can do it by ourselves; we do not need God. It seeks to make answers to the most complex of human problems very simple, and can therefore appear an attractive way to follow.

Thetans are the life force or spirit. Originally they were uncreated gods but are now incarnated into human lives. They are basically good but are handicapped by the existence of the *engram*, which is received when the person in past lives has experienced physical or emotional pain.

People who are being recruited into Scientology are known as *preclear* because of the faults within them. They are tested by the *E-meter* – or electropsychometer. This is the instrument by which answers to the personality questionnaire are emotionally registered so that the *auditor* can determine the characteristics of the *preclear*.

The Auditor is the representative from the 'church' who is asking the questions or giving the commands. The process of *Auditing* is to enable the preclear to come to a place of *clear*.

Auditing is a long and expensive process in which the auditor interviews the preclear. The auditor will talk about the past until the engram is removed. Results from the E-meter are calculated and the relevant courses are then sold in order for the person to become clear. Estimates vary from £12,000-£30,000 needed to take you through the 100 steps and 64 levels to the clear state. These steps are fully described in a 1982 Scientology publication, *From Clear to Eternity.*

According to the Associated Press, court documents reveal that the Church of Scientology belief goes like this: Seventy-five million years ago, Earth was actually called *Teegeeach*. It was ruled - along with some 90 other planets - by *Xetnu*, who spread his evil by blowing up the world with nuclear bombs. Survivors from this attack were inhabited by spirits from another planet (thetans).

Always Being Ready!

Humans today are derived from these thetans and are basically good. The thetans have evolved upwards to humans and do not now remember their former state. To allow the full potential of the thetans to be released, the engram needs to be audited. As you are audited and become clear, the dormant thetan-state in you is awakened.

As with other cults under this heading, one of the most worrying aspects, as we indicated above, is not just what they believe but the way that they treat people. Scientologists have a policy of 'Fair Game'. This is the process by which the individual is harassed, defamed and has embarrassing information sent to friends, colleagues, press, etc. Justice Latey says that 'Fair Game' may cause:

> "... deprival of property, injury by any means, trickery, suing, lying or destruction ... He then goes on to give two clear proven illustrations of this."

Many leave Scientology broken people. We need to understand and befriend them. We may need to pass them on to others for expert help, and they need our love and care to help them be restored.

The ostrich mentality

These opening chapters have sought to give an understanding of the world of the cults in Britain. It is not a pretty picture, but we must deal with the real world. We can play the proverbial ostrich and pretend it is not happening, but that will not alter the facts. Legislation will not curb the cults. Hateful demonstrations will not free people. The loving, patient, and powerful witness of a Christian is the only answer.

Having painted the picture, we are ready to move on. How can I be ready to be used in this battle? How can I be safe in Christ and simultaneously be effective in my witnessing to these people?

Section 2
Overview of God's Work in us
6 - Know the Truth

A preacher friend of mine told me once that the Word of God
is like an eternal loaf of bread. No matter how many slices
you cut off there will always be enough left to feed you.
Probably not even the greatest saint has ever plumbed the
depth or seen every facet of God's Word.

The Bible tells us that a time will come when God's
people will not want to listen to the Word of God. They will
prefer to have their ears tickled by the latest fad (2 Timothy
4:3-4). Paul even mentioned that people would accumulate
their own particular teachers who matched their desires, and
in so doing would accept myths rather than the truth.

I cannot help but note in passing that this is so
descriptive of much of the 'church' scene today. Fads are
everywhere to be found and unless you have read the latest
book, been blessed in the latest way or seen the latest
manifestation you can hardly call yourself a Christian. At the
same time, the exposition of God's Word is giving way to
multi-media presentations and sound-bites that cannot even
feed a sparrow, let alone a fully fledged Christian.

I believe, however, that once the famine caused by the
lack of God's sound doctrine is apparent, there will again be a
hunger and thirst for the truth. I hope we are somewhere
within this transition period.

We have been moving through the days when, in some
fellowships, the Bible has become secondary to worship and
the gifts. The so-called "Toronto Blessing" had this effect in
some churches, where the exposition of God's Word was put
aside for 'carpet time'. Do not misunderstand me – we need
worship; we need gifts; we need times when God touches us;
and we need to show that Christianity is attractive, but not at

71

the expense of God's Word. Luke 11:52 tells us of the lawyers who not only did not enter the reality of God's Word themselves but they also took the opportunity away from others. We need those today who will faithfully preach and open the way for all to enter the reality of the teaching of Scripture.

Getting caught up with the latest fad is rather like the Doctor that only ever prescribes a certain drug for whatever illness is presented by the patient. In 'x' cases out of 10 he is right and the patient improves but in all the others the main root of the disease goes undetected and the patient might even get worse.

Looking back over 40 years of my Christian life, I have seen many fads come and go and each of them, in the end, has removed people from the reality of God's Word and left them relying on the teaching built up by the man or group. For some it appeared to work, but for many it left them disturbed and disappointed – had God really let them down?

I remember phases such as – whatever the case, just praise the Lord and all will be well - then there was covenant relationship, followed by many others. Today, many of the fads are to do with counselling; they are not necessarily wrong in *every* case but they cannot be applied to all without wisdom.

Generational Curses

Generational curses are an example of this today. A full discussion of this subject is available in a Reachout Trust Fact File, but here I quote two paragraphs to give one reason why I believe this is a 'fad':

> "Another significant general observation I want to make is concerning Jesus' ministry. More than anyone else Jesus dealt with demonic cases, and yet in all the records there is not one hint of 'Generational Curses'. Indeed, the one time that Jesus could have easily taught about the matter, in John 9:1-3,

He made clear that the 'curse' had nothing to do with the past.

"This leads me to ask the question as to whether the emphasis that has developed on 'Generational Curses' in the last few years is a real or an imagined one? Is it the latest fad of which we have had so many in the past years, or is there clear Biblical teaching that shows that we are experiencing today an unprecedented revival in these areas? Ten years ago you hardly heard about them, today just about everyone has a curse according to some Bible teachers."

Revelation Teaching

Another problem faced today is 'revelation teaching' or maybe one could term them 'gimmicks' which by definition is, "adapted for the purpose of attracting attention or publicity". The preacher can say whatever he likes as long as he says that God revealed it to him and usually it is to draw attention to himself and ministry, rather than a true exposition of the Word of God.

I remember friends coming to our stand at Eurofire in Birmingham a number of years ago. They had just left a seminar where Benny Hinn (see p.44) had rewritten Genesis chapters 1–3 on the basis that God had given him direct revelation. My friends were shell-shocked that anyone could do such a thing but, since then Benny Hinn, among others, has often repeated this method of teaching, even telling his audience once that there were nine members of the Trinity.

I am aware that Hinn retracted that statement but how could a Bible Student ever make the mistake in the first place? Indeed, how can someone who loves the Lord and claims to be His true servant say, and indeed do, many of the things captured on video and tape? Benny Hinn is a man that has been caught out in doctrinal error several times. A man that has been accused of telling lies and can bring no clear defence other than it is all conspiracy against him as a man of God. A man that claims to have a very special anointing from God but has made clear false prophecies under this anointing – does God make such mistakes? Nevertheless, he is talked of as a man of God, pastoring a church of thousands; appearing regularly on television and held as one of the leading men of God today. Our conclusion from the facts would be that this is a gimmick and many people have been caught up with Benny Hinn and others just like him. Much of what they do is a myth and a smokescreen of showmanship, but folks do not want to speak out or move away because others are saying he is a man of God.

A third problem area arises when people believe only what their leaders reveal as truth. This can become cult-like and does not allow young Christians the opportunity to grow up and meditate on the Scriptures themselves. They believe things that they have not checked out with the whole word of God. The 'end-times triumphalist teaching of The Manifest Sons of God' gains ground in this way. This teaching says that the church will be ruling and reigning on the earth and that will bring Jesus back. Does the Bible really teach that? Christians in some groups have no opportunity to find out.

Manifest Sons of God

Many are influenced by this teaching that has many names, such as, The Latter Rain Movement, Identity, Joel's Army, Restoration and Reconstruction. The Scriptures refer to the rains in Israel as the 'former rain', essential for planting and the 'latter rain', needed for the harvest. Manifest Sons see the former rain as Pentecost and the latter rain a greater outpouring of the Spirit in these last days. There is evidence that much teaching on spiritual warfare today is largely an extension of this doctrine.

All Scriptures that refer to a resurrection or redemption of the body are to be fulfilled by a select group of overcomers, the Sons of God, while here on earth. They believe that they will be sinless and immortal in their physical bodies when they become Manifest as the Sons of God. All Scriptures that refer to being caught up to the throne of God are thought to have their fulfillment at this Manifestation of the Sons of God, the "many-membered man child" company that will rule the nations with a rod of iron.

They will become Christ both corporately and individually. They consider the corporate body of Christ, to be Christ. The body of Christ is thought to be a literal extension of the incarnation of Christ. This causes both Scriptures that refer to His ruling the nations and judging the world to find fulfillment through them.

A distinction is made between Christ's coming to rule and judge the world through the Sons of God and His later individual, personal return. He is unable to return until the stage is set by the establishment of His rule and reign through the Sons of God subduing the nations, or taking dominion, and executing judgment on the ungodly, thus establishing the new age.

Jesus is considered the 'Pattern Son'. He was the first one to make it as a divine, immortal, sinless Manifest Son of God and this accomplishment will be duplicated by each individual who following Jesus become Manifest Sons of God. This Christ Company, now individually Manifest as Sons of God, will execute judgment at the Great and Terrible Day of the Lord.

For many William Branham is regarded as the greatest prophet for this 'final age'. Yet there were many errors in Branham's teachings along with occult influences, including having the voice of an angel talking to him regularly and who often would 'heal through him'.

George Warnock's book *The Feast of Tabernacles*, written in 1951, became an important part of the Latter Rain Movement and it continues to be used today. According to Warnock, the feasts of Israel, described in Leviticus 23, are a pattern for the progress of the church. Starting at Passover, which is Calvary, the church has passed through the different feasts to Pentecost. It must go on through the Day of Atonement, the Feast of Trumpets and culminate in the Feast of Tabernacles, which many believe is fulfilled in the 'present revival'.

Earl Paulk, Pastor and called 'Archbishop' of Cathedral at Chapel Hill Church, Atlanta, Georgia, (http://www.col.tv/) is recognized as a modern-day 'prophet', and Rick Joyner is another teacher for this movement. He believes that the elite 'overcomers' will conquer the world. This will lead to the greatest revival of history, where the majority of the world will be won to Christ and the kingdom made ready to be received by Christ.

The concept of Christ has been changed. In the orthodox reading of Scripture, Jesus of Nazareth, one person, is the Christ – the Lord's anointed. This is changed so that, the Body of Christ, *is* Christ! Therefore, what Scriptures say that Jesus Christ will accomplish, is now to be accomplished by the 'man-Christ.' The Sons of God now do the work, not Jesus. This is a 'different Jesus' from the one my Bible speaks of. He is the one that will do the work, not men.

We are not dealing here with one organization, but with belief and philosophy. A philosophy that teaches that the church is Christ in a corporate sense, and it that undertakes responsibilities that the Bible says are reserved for Jesus Christ. Not everyone goes to the same extremes, but the basic beliefs that lead to extremes are common.

In other groups, you must firmly believe that God has finished with his people, Israel, and the church is now the Israel of God. No difference from the group's teaching can be accepted, and so it's not worth studying the Scriptures.

Replacement Theology

The roots of Replacement Theology go back to the early Church and became the seed bed of 'Christian anti-Semitism.' It teaches that:

1. Israel has been replaced by the Christian Church in the purposes of God. The Church is now the continuation of Israel and the latter is excluded. After Pentecost 'Israel', in the Bible, refers only to the Church.

2. The Jewish people are now no longer God's chosen people and the promises, covenants and blessings ascribed to Israel in the Bible have been taken away from the Jews and given to the Church. The Jews are subject, however, to the curses found in the Bible.

3. The Jewish people as a whole have no specific future, hope, nor calling in God's economy. Individual Jews can be saved.

Scriptural verses used to teach Replacement Theology include: **Matthew 21:43** and similar verses: Jesus says that the kingdom of God would be taken away from the Jews. However, these verses must be read in context as Jesus was not talking to the whole race of Israel but specifically to the Pharisees, chief priests, etc.

Romans 2:28-29 is dealing with the fact that, whatever we believe, it must be from the heart and not just an outward show. Relationship is the key. This has nothing to do with one group replacing another, rather it shows that both are on the same footing.

Romans 11:17-23 talks about the Gentiles being grafted *into* the original olive tree *not* replacing it. It shows that the Gentiles are drawing on the same life

Verses such as **Galatians 3:29 and Romans 4:13** are used to show that Abraham only had a partial inheritance but the church today has the fullness. However, these and similar verses in the New Testament do not *exclude* Israel but rather *include* the Gentiles. Gentiles have been brought in to the fulfillment of the promises of God, not Israel excluded and replaced.

Other Verses to consider

Ephesians 2:11-18 are central to this subject, and they show clearly that replacement theology is not taught within

Always Being Ready!

Scripture. They do not just show that the Jews need the Gentiles but, equally for fullness, the Gentiles need the Jews. Note the following statements that are made in these verses.

- We were excluded from the commonwealth of Israel
- We were strangers to the covenant of promise
- Now Christ's purpose is to make the two into one
- Now He wants to establish peace
- Access to God is the same for both parties.

Clearly it is talking about a *unity* of two groups, not a *takeover* by one of them!

Romans 11:11-36 reveals that indeed for a time the Jews did stumble in order that the Gentiles may come in. But within the verses there is a clear warning not to be smug about what has happened because God has not yet finished with Israel; indeed God's dealings with Israel are everlasting.

These teachings are a misrepresentation of Scripture, but if an individual is not allowed to question the leader making the statements, we accept the error and do not do as we are told by the Lord and check it out with Scripture. However, there is also a level of this that seems to be even more dangerous. It is bad enough to believe wrong doctrine but, when that doctrine can have disastrous consequences in your life, you have come across a spoof, which means that such teaching is a swindle or a hoax; a parody of the truth.

An example of this is the teaching and the publicity of the John Avanzini Ministries. In a mass produced *Reader's Digest*-style letter, that unfortunately many use today, he writes:

> "The Lord directed me to get this letter to you as quickly as possible. ... This morning as I was praying ... I sensed in my spirit that you or someone close to you is facing a financial crisis. Is this true?"

Surely, this sort of statement is more at home in clairvoyance than the gospel of Jesus Christ. Indeed, many mediums and psychics send out similar letters. Avanzini then begins to relate the story of the feeding of the 5,000 and ends with this advice:

> "When you take what you have ... give it to God, and ask Him to bless it ... you are taking your problem of insufficiency out of the natural realm and releasing it to the supernatural for a solution."

We can see where this is leading and surely it does not come from the Lord. However, before he blatantly tells them to give the money to him, we read one more scripture:

> "Just as I finishing this letter to you, I felt impressed of the Lord to look at Matthew 16:19: '... and whatsoever you bind on earth will be bound in Heaven, and whatsoever you loose on earth will be loosed in Heaven.' Right then, I saw that the word 'whatsoever' includes YOUR MONEY!"

Not only is he taking words out of context, but surely he is saying that God says things He does not – this is nearer blasphemy than God's ministry.

I wonder what Avanzini does with all the money sent to him from people who cannot afford it, and who end up further in debt because they are relying on a spoof rather than the Word of God. This type of ministry brings God's name into disrepute.

Fortunately, God's Word also gives us instruction how to deal with such issues and be able to walk safely in Him. First, we should note that 1 Kings 13 gives us a clear warning of the consequences when the prophet listened to what man said instead of what God said.

> "Now it came about, as they were sitting down at the table, that the word of the LORD came to the prophet who had brought him back; and he cried to the man of God who came from

Always Being Ready!

> Judah, saying, 'Thus says the LORD, "Because you have disobeyed the command of the LORD, and have not observed the commandment which the LORD your God commanded you, but have returned and eaten bread and drunk water in the place of which He said to you, 'Eat no bread and drink no water'; your body shall not come to the grave of your fathers."'" – 1 Kings 13:20-22

This may be an extreme case but the warning is clear: if a man tells you to do something other than God tells you, do not do it. We have no one else to blame; it is our responsibility to check the message against all of God's word.

Added to this, 1 Kings 22 relates the time when the kings of Israel and Judah went out to fight together and various prophets were brought before them. Most said what they thought the kings wanted to hear and were false prophets. But the warning is still there for the hearer: do not just listen to the messages we like and ignore the rest.

1 John 4:1 teaches us not to believe every spirit, but test the spirits to see if they come from God. We should not automatically believe every doctrine that is said to be the revelation of the Spirit of God, or every teacher who claims to speak under His anointing.

The testing is not by human reason, but by the Word of God, which is the standard of all doctrine; whatever agrees with that is to be received, and what does not should be rejected. The Bereans in Acts 17:11 were commended for the way they examined the Scriptures, even when Paul spoke! In the letter to Ephesus (Revelation 2:2) they are commended for putting to the test the false apostles. We need to judge for ourselves, to test the spirits, but also respect the Body of Christ of which we are part.

Theology

The teachings and actions described above have left many young Christians without the desire to study the Word of

God. Some are even without the ability, and many are
without the foundation that is necessary if they are to grow in
the Christian life. Theology has gone out of fashion. I was
very fortunate to grow up spiritually in a fellowship where
the Word of God was expounded and preached faithfully; I
am so glad, too, that my involvement with cult work has
forced me back into the study of God's Word. As I hear each
cult argument, it causes me to go to find the truth. The forged
£20 note illustration used in chapter 1 is very relevant. As
every forgery comes across our path, let it cause us to study
the original in greater detail. We will then know why the false
is false and, more than that, we can show others why. Paul
encouraged Timothy (I Timothy 4:6) to be constantly
nourished by sound doctrine and to be a good servant and
point these things out to others. This verse is for us too.

E. H. Bancroft, in his *Introduction to Christian Theology*
writes that theology is necessary for four reasons:

1. "Theology is necessary as a means of
   expressing the meaning of Christianity
   because man is reasonable as well as
   emotional.
2. It is necessary in order to define Christianity.
   The definitions may not be exhaustive, for the
   objects and experiences involved are beyond
   our capacity for knowing, in some of their
   aspects. But we may apprehend what we can
   not comprehend. We may know in part not in
   full. We may know truly if not exhaustively.
3. It is necessary in order to defend Christianity
   against attack.
4. It is necessary in order to propagate it.
   Christianity is a missionary religion: it is
   aggressive and diffusive in motive and aim.
   But no possible success can attend the
   propagation of Christianity without doctrine.
   The truth is employed to produce experience,
   then experience gives a new appreciation of
   truth." – p.14.

Always Being Ready!

These definitions show just how important theology is for us in our task of reaching the cults. In view of this, it is tragic that so many seem only interested in the power and believe that theology is dead. Watching the old steam trains at Minehead made me think what would happen if the powerful engines were to come off the rails and charge down the High Street. The track that keeps that beautiful and powerful engine going in a straight line is vital. Yes, we can have the power today – we need the power today – but not just to be let loose without direction. Theology is the track that enables the power to run without causing damage or mayhem in people's lives. God by His Spirit never does anything that is contrary to the Word He has spoken. After all, the Word was breathed out by the same Holy Spirit and He is not schizophrenic!

There is no substitute for the Word of God delivered in the power and safety of the Holy Spirit. The dead letter kills and we should not be using it in such a way. Teaching of the Word of God should be empowered and enabled by the Holy Spirit, and then it will bring life. There is no substitute for theology, whatever we are doing in the Christian life, and more so when dealing with the cults.

As I said, I had a very good grounding in the Word of God from the moment I became a Christian but when the Lord called me into cult work I found that I was forced back into the Word of God. Would the earth last for ever and we live on it? Who were the 144,000? Was the Trinity doctrine created by the pagans? These and many other questions sent me back to see what the Bible had to say. If we are to communicate clearly and simply with those in the cults, we must have a solid foundation in the Word of God. Paul's instruction to Timothy was to be diligent and handle accurately the word of truth (1 Timothy 2:15).

Errors creep in

Errors will appear when the Word of God is not treated as very important. The sin of the Israelites during the captivity in Babylon is testimony to this. When they were to return to the land we find in Ezra and Nehemiah that the study of the Word of God (Ezra 7:10), reading (Nehemiah 8:1-8), and obedience to (Nehemiah 13:1-3) was vital to the restoration. The Book of Chronicles is often a seesaw story of good king, bad king, good king. Jehoshophat was one of those who sought to walk with the Lord. We find in 2 Chronicles 17:9 that one of the first things he did was to send out his officials to teach the people the Law of the Lord. We could multiply these examples many times over; they all emphasise the fact that the Word of God is vital.

In 2 Timothy 3:15 Paul reminds Timothy that he has known the sacred writings since his youth and that these lead to wisdom and salvation. They are vital because they are for teaching, correction and training. No wonder errors creep in if we move away from the revealed Word of God. No wonder there can be a problem if we add some ceremony or idea that has no foundation in Scripture at all. No wonder we fall into error if we want God to speak directly to us when His written word has already made the matter plain. When we move away from the Bible as our basis, we miss God's teaching, correction and training, and so errors must come in.

Many of you will be in churches where the Word of God is taught faithfully and you will be receiving the grounding you need. If not, then you might need to supplement what you are receiving by studying yourself. You will find some great study aids to help you in your local Christian bookshop. Do not be fooled into thinking that it does not matter. Remember the story of the wise man and the foolish man in Matthew 7:24-27. Unless we hear the Word of God and *act upon it* we are simply building on sand. The building will survive in the calm weather but the moment the storm tests it the building will be no more. We may appear to be fine in calm weather but there is nothing like the storm of the cults to test our faith. At Reachout we have tragic stories on file of those who felt they were strong, but because there was no real grounding, they were shipwrecked by the constant questioning and disagreement of the cults. Every Christian is a potential mission field for the cults and eventually you will be tested, so ensure that you have the grounding to stand.

Real to me

This parable also explains why there are some people who have heard the Word of God for years but who are still not growing or able to stand: our calling is not to be hearers only, but also *doers* of the word. We can hear God speaking but, as the parable of the sower or, probably more correctly, the parable of the soils (Mark 4:1-20) shows, we can allow other things to take its place. The same Word is sown in each case; it is the receptiveness that changes, not the seed. There are two other very interesting facts in this parable.

First, if the seed is sown in good ground it is a definite promise that it *will* bear fruit; yes, of differing amounts, but to the full capacity of the one in whom it is sown. Second, Satan knows just how important the reception of the Word is because he has three plans to get rid of it. Satan would not bother this much if it wasn't so important. Sometimes I even think that Satan is more aware of the importance and power of God's Word than we are.

If we are to be strong in God then we need reality. We will not just believe what someone else has said but we will have experienced the reality of that Word ourselves. From our lips will come not the third-hand information about Jesus Whom Paul preaches, but the reality of Jesus within our lives. Think back to Luke 11:52. The problem was that the lawyers had not 'entered in', and they were hindering those who wanted to enter the reality of God's Word.

We need both to hear the Word of God and also to act on it. We need to listen attentively to what others are saying but then also know the work of the Holy Spirit making that message real in our lives. Without these steps we are not allowing Scripture to have full effect in our lives. This is probably the one area in which we need to be selfish. Paul told Timothy to pay attention to himself first and then give out to others (1 Timothy 4:16). If the Word of God is not worked out in reality in our lives, then we will not be much help to others.

What about me?

In the area of the cults, probably the most important question we need answered from Scripture is: Am I safe when dealing with them? The Bible is clear on this matter but if we have never seen it then we will have doubts and fears. These doubts and fears, in Satan's usual way, will be based on fiction rather than fact. However, once we have the solid ground of the Word of God under our feet we can be strong.

We need to go back to the beginning. The foundation for our position as we seek to help those who have been blinded by Satan is found in Genesis 1:1: "In the beginning God ..." No one else was there: no other heavenly creation and certainly no earthly creation. God was there alone! I often say that one of the greatest helps in spiritual warfare is to picture a totally blank piece of paper with just one word written at the top: God. He is all-supreme and no other being in heaven or on earth can match Him. He is the only one who is omnipresent, everywhere, all the time. He is the only one who knows everything and can control everything. Some Christians want to give these attributes to Satan but his position is seen when we read Psalm 148:1-6; God created all heavenly things, including the angels. In other words, God created the angel who was to rebel and become Satan. God is clearly more powerful than Satan ever was. Satan's fall is recorded in Isaiah 14:12-15 and Ezekiel 28:12-19. No one can lift their hand against God and win.

After the heavenly creation, we read that God created the earth. The heavenly creation was supernatural but the human was natural. Clearly, then, as a human I am not stronger than Satan because he is heavenly and I am earthly. No wonder he can deceive and manipulate this human race; he is greater than we are! But remember, before you start panicking, that Satan is not greater than God. As I give my will over to

Christ and allow Him to be Lord, He takes control. Satan no longer has to contend with a mere human being but Christ in me. Is Satan stronger than Christ in me? No! As Christians we are stronger because Satan is subject to Christ. James 4:7 puts it in a nutshell. This verse does not just say that if we resist the devil he will flee; that would not be scriptural! What it does say is, "Submit yourselves ... to God. Resist the devil, and he will flee from you." The promise of God's Word is that as I am subject to Christ in my life, the devil must flee as I resist him. Not because I am great but because Christ in me has already won the victory. This is our position in Christ. If this is reality to us then we can approach the cults not with fear and trepidation but with that humble assurance of who we are in Christ.

Over to you

Do be encouraged to find out the joys of studying the Word of God for yourself. First, it will build you up and you will learn what God wants to reveal to you. Secondly, you will be able to communicate what you find to others. This is the way to study Scripture – allow God to speak to you so that you can speak to others.

Seeing truth from God's Word and allowing God to make it real in our lives is step one; we then need to express it with the right attitude. Hitting someone over the head with a 'heavy word' is not the way. The Word of God is described in Ephesians 6 as the 'sword of the Spirit'. He is the one who will enable us to use the Scriptures with tact and finesse but without losing its power. He is the one who will enable us to build bridges and yet still convey what God thinks about the cult group. It is not always easy; we need to look at the work of the Holy Spirit in our preparation for reaching out to the cults. Chapters 9 and 10 will build on this foundation and will outline some of the central Biblical beliefs for an evangelical Christian.

7 - Know the Life

It had been a traumatic few weeks for the small band of followers. Their leader had been killed and they had to hide because of the persecution. Feeling scared and vulnerable, they had seen their leader walk through the wall of their upstairs room, several days after He had died, and eat with them. Now they were standing on a hillside talking to two angels after they had seen their leader rising into heaven and out of sight through the clouds. No one would ever believe them!

However, that was not the immediate worry of this small group; it was Jesus' last words that had rooted them to the spot. Trying to find out exactly what would happen, and when they would be free from Roman occupation, they had asked Him about the setting up of His kingdom. He had mentioned it often but surely it was now or never. Maybe the latter, because, according to His answer that was not for them to know, but still what He said caused consternation.

When the Holy Spirit came upon them, they would be His witnesses. They would have no option, other than to be a good witness or a bad witness. When the Lord sent the Holy Spirit to be with them He would testify of Jesus and so their lives would be bound up with Him. Yet there was more; "You will be my witnesses in Jerusalem ..." That was a little bit frightening because of all the persecution that had been going on, although at least they could speak to people who understood them and would probably be sympathetic. "... And in all Judea ..." was a challenge, but they would still be dealing with people they would feel at home with. Then the bombshells started to drop: "... and in Samaria ..."; that could not be, because Jews have no dealings with the Samaritans. How on earth can we ever tell them? And if we do, what will the people in Jerusalem say? Still there was worse: "... and to the ends of the earth." That was in the hands of the Gentiles.

It would be bad enough speaking to the Samaritans, but witnessing to the Gentiles as well!

Always Being Ready!

I hope you get the picture of the shock that these disciples must have felt. Nothing had ever happened like the events that they witnessed and now they were being told to do things that no Jew had ever done before. It is a lesson that we need to learn when dealing with the cults. We may feel that many cults are just like the Samaritans to the Jews – we have no dealings with them. We may feel they are like the Gentiles, those who do not deserve to receive the gospel of grace. But the fact remains that we have been chosen to be witnesses to them. The only option will be whether we will witness to them of the true love and grace of God, or show them hatred and persecution. Either way we will be witnesses, and either way they will react to what they see and hear from our witness.

God's enabler

The Holy Spirit is part of the Godhead and He needs to be treated and respected as God. We must never lose sight of the fact of who He is and what the Scriptures reveal about Him. Ephesians chapter 1 gives us a picture of the Godhead. Verses 3-4 show us that the Father is the originator; verses 4-12 show that Jesus is the One who makes it all possible; and verses 13-14 show us that the Holy Spirit is the One who equips and makes it real within the lives of God's children. That is His ministry to us today. The fullness of our salvation has not yet been revealed but it will come because of the Holy Spirit within our lives.

We may not always feel that we are filled to overflowing; the widow who spoke to Elisha certainly did not (2 Kings 4.) She had to be reminded that she had the small jar of oil tucked away in some dark cupboard. Then she was encouraged to use it under the direction of Elijah, and what a miracle! The small amount of oil became a houseful. Oil in the Old Testament is a picture of the Holy Spirit. Sometimes we only have a small amount tucked away somewhere but we need to pour it out at the Lord's command. We too will find it will keep pouring until the need is met.

The Holy Spirit also distributes gifts as He pleases (1 Corinthians 12:11). These enable us to bring the reality of the life of God to people in this world. Tapping into God's knowledge is not just so we can do some spiritual party trick, but so that God can reveal something that will bring glory to His Name. Speaking in prophecy is not just so you will know which job to go after or home to buy. Prophecy is God speaking directly into people's situations and affecting them by His life. I would not say that it is essential to know the gifts of the Holy Spirit when speaking to cult members, but we should note that usually they are a tremendous asset.

Some cults say that the gifts of the Holy Spirit are not for today: they were only necessary to see the early church established or until that which is perfect, the Bible, came into being. This last thought comes from 1 Corinthians 13:10 which says that when that which is perfect comes, the gifts that are partial will cease. But, what is "that which is perfect" and, more to the point, has it 'come'? The Bible is the Word of God, but I do not believe it is what is described by the phrase, "that which is perfect". There is still a greater revelation for us when God sets up His kingdom; the Bible indeed foretells that one day this fullness will be reality. When we see the Lord face to face we will not need the gifts, but until then they reveal God to the people, and we should be seeking the Lord to release them through us for ministry to the cults – among other things.

Love, patience and faithfulness are often qualities needed when dealing with cult members and these are shown to be fruits of the Holy Spirit. We may have a measure of these things in our own personality but eventually that will be exhausted. Remember, though, God's great 'Enabler' never tires and He can continue to provide these qualities beyond our own resources. Welcome the Holy Spirit into your life and give Him the opportunity to produce the fruits. Fruit is not just for you to hold and say how wonderful it looks. Fruit is to be tasted. Those in the cults will see the fruit of the Holy Spirit in you and will want to taste and see what it is.

Always Being Ready!

We need the ministry of the Holy Spirit if we are to talk to the cults. He is the One Who provides the power for the steam train to run on the track of God's Word. If you have not taken enough notice of the Third Person of the Trinity until now, do take this opportunity to seek God. Ask the Lord that He will give you a greater awareness of this Person of the Godhead and will reveal His vital work in your life. Please be encouraged by Luke 11:13 where we are told that the Father will give the Holy Spirit to those who ask. We certainly needed to know the work of the Holy Spirit when we first accepted Christ, but there is also an ongoing ministry for every day of our Christian lives. Let us ask God to minister through us to others.

Let us now look at some specific ways that He will help us as we prepare to reach out to those in the cults.

The changing work of the Holy Spirit

If you are perfect, you have my permission to skip this section. All still here? Good! Most Christians are aware that they are not perfect and that changes are needed. In the area of communicating to the cults I find I need the Holy Spirit to make several things real in my life. He also has to change the way I do things. I can look back in my life to at least two occasions where God has had to bring me down to the ground. We cannot be used if we think we are the greatest thing since Balaam's ass. We cannot be used if we just go blundering on like Elijah running away from that still, small voice. Even with the earthquake, thunder and lightning going on around us, we need the peace of God within to enable us to listen. The Holy Spirit needs to teach us these lessons. Sometimes the lessons are hard because we are determined to go our own way. The Holy Spirit brings a 'softness' to our personalities although we are not 'softies'. He brings gentleness in the way we say the hardest things. These qualities are vital as we get ready to speak to the cult member.

James 1:19 highlights the pre-eminent quality of communication that we need the Holy Spirit to make real in our lives – and this has nothing to do with speaking. We are told to be quick to hear and slow to speak. We have two ears and one mouth and we need to use them in that proportion. So much can be accomplished as we listen to people telling us about themselves. The Holy Spirit can give us an insight into the character behind the words. If we have our pat answer ready and two minutes after the cultist has started, we are telling him the way to solve all his problems, I doubt if we are under the guidance of the Holy Spirit. Many are ready to shout, "Jesus is the answer", before anyone has asked a question. Many have learnt the appropriate Scripture and the appropriate counsel for each situation they come across. This does not work. We are not talking about static situations but about living people and each person will be different. We need to allow the Holy Spirit to teach us to be quiet and let him do the talking when He is ready.

We are not to condone wrong attitudes and beliefs of cultists, yet at the same time we are not to condemn them, for what may be genuine reasons, for being in the cult. We must not put standards on them that God has not put on us. Hebrews 4:14 – 5:10 shows us that our High Priest can both understand us and sympathise with our weaknesses. These may not be qualities that come naturally to us, but they are qualities that the Holy Spirit can reveal in us. They are also vital qualities if we are truly going to help people be set free.

Victims of the cults need to be shown lots of love and care. They need to experience compassion and restoration. Our care for people will often have to go beyond just the initial 'preaching of the gospel'. If they come to our church we may be helping them for many months. They may have said and done things of which they are now ashamed, or other Christians may have condemned them for what they have done. A few platitudes are not the answer. We need to meditate on Jesus' treatment of Peter in John 21. There are clear indications that Jesus was deliberately reminding Peter

– and maybe the others – of the night of the betrayal. The fire will have reminded Peter of the fire he stood beside and denied his Lord. Interestingly, the Greek word for "fire" in those two instances is the same and these are the only times that word is used in Scripture. Three times the Lord asked Peter if he loved Him, reminding Peter of the three denials. Jesus did not do it to condemn but rather to show the restoration work that God wanted to do in Peter's life. Cult members have probably said and done many things that they now regret. Many may have even misrepresented Christ and persecuted Christians – as Paul did. And just as the Lord received and restored Peter and Paul, so we are to welcome and help these former cult members.

I cannot emphasise this quality of the Holy Spirit enough. John 16:8 tells us that the Holy Spirit will convict, not condemn. As those filled with the Holy Spirit, we will not have a ministry of condemnation, but the Spirit will move through us to convict the sinner. Condemnation says, "You have sinned and you have had it!" Conviction says, "You have sinned and this is the way out." The Holy Spirit will convict these people but not condemn them.

Communication of the Holy Spirit

We should continually be learning lessons about the Holy Spirit's enabling, although I'm sure we will never get perfect in one area before He moves us on to another. While our education continues, we can begin to learn about the next stage too. Having come to recognise at least the basics in our character that need to be changed, having 'got into negotiation' with God to do the work by the Holy Spirit, we can now look at the next step. In the last section we talked about our inward attitudes to these people and the need to be silent and listen. Now we need to look at what we are to say when we open our mouth.

In our seminars at Reachout Trust, we teach various presentations that can be used with the different cults. We give no five-year guarantees and we also urge people not to rely just on the plans; it is the Holy Spirit who will convict a person of what is wrong and what is right. If we ever get to the stage of thinking that pointing out a specific verse in a particular way will mean that a person will come to Christ, we are going to be disappointed. The purpose of the presentations is to offer the best way of sharing the gospel with the cultists. Their minds only think in certain ways and they have all sorts of protective mechanisms to prevent any serious questions getting through to them.

Jesus would often ask questions to get through this barrier. In Luke 10:25 we find a lawyer standing up to put Jesus to the test. Jesus, knowing what was going on, does not turn him away but answers his question with another question that reveals much to the man. Mark 11:27-33 reveals again Jesus' way of asking questions. Knowing that whatever answer He gave to the question of authority, it would have been misused, He asked a simple question about the baptism of John. They scribes and elders would not answer Jesus because they did not like the truth and they knew that whatever they said would backfire on them; as a result, neither did Jesus answer their question. Asking questions can often reveal something to the person that no amount of accusation would bring.

Our presentations are similar; we want to make the person look at something in a different light so that all their standard alarms and protection mechanisms are switched off. With their power source disconnected, a new source can come online and the Holy Spirit will have a way into their life. But again, I would urge you to use presentations, but not rely on them. Rely on the fact that the Holy Spirit can use what is being said; He can bring freshness to a message that these people have been told is not for them.

Most of those in the cults are still not 'born again' of God's Holy Spirit and they are still looking at the things of God, with what Paul describes as 'the natural mind'. He also tells us that the natural mind does not understand the things of God (1 Corinthians 2:14). How, then, are we to get through to such people? We read that we need to have spiritual words to express spiritual thoughts (1 Corinthians 2:13). This is the work of the Holy Spirit in and through us.

Teaching of the Holy Spirit

John 16:13 tells us clearly that it is the work of the Holy Spirit to lead into all truth. He may use us but it is His job and we can trust Him to do it in His time and His way. I remember an incident with one of the first Jehovah's Witnesses that I led to the Lord. She was coming very close to receiving Christ as her Saviour but had a real problem about the Trinity. A succinct and helpful answer was needed. I felt the Holy Spirit prompt me to say, "Don't worry about it; it doesn't matter for now." Although I said it, feeling it was from the Lord, I did worry about it on the way home. I only stopped worrying when I remembered that on the night I came to Christ I did not believe or understand the Trinity. I did not even know that Jesus was God! At that time it did not matter. What did matter was that I knew that Jesus was God's sacrifice for sin and that if I truly repented I could be saved. A few weeks later, after this woman had come to Christ, I was greeted with a broad smile when I knocked on her door. She told me excitedly that she had been reading her Bible and had seen the Trinity on every page! This is the work of the Holy Spirit.

I learnt some lessons from this incident. First, it is the Holy Spirit's job to lead us into all truth. He has been doing it far longer and does it far better than we ever can. Commit the people you are dealing with firmly into His hands. Secondly, we are not to put conditions on people that God does not put on us. He does not demand that we fully understand the Trinity before we accept Him. We should not expect every cult member to get all their theology right before they repent and receive Christ. Sometimes it will take many months or years to do all that. This leads me to the third lesson; it is according to the Holy Spirit's timing and plans that these things are dealt with. My job is to encourage cult members to trust themselves fully to God. This gives the Holy Spirit the opportunity to work at His pace, and in His way, within their lives.

Leading of the Holy Spirit

Under this final heading I want to emphasise something we mentioned earlier in the chapter – the still, small voice within. Some of you will never have experienced a word of knowledge, but that does not mean that you never will. Some may think they have never made a prophetic statement that has brought the reality of God directly into the life of someone else, but there is always a first time. These gifts of the Holy Spirit are often stereotyped in our minds and that is partly why we do not experience them. We may think you have to be a preacher at the end of the meeting to get a word of knowledge about those who need healing or deliverance. The prophetic word must come in a booming voice, go on for several minutes and end or begin with, 'Thus says the Lord'. These gifts may come like this, but that is not the only way. If we restrict them in this manner then we could be missing out on knowing the Holy Spirit at work in our lives.

Having learned all the rights and wrongs of what to do with cult members, and having learnt a great presentation and underlined all the relevant Scriptures, you may feel you are ready and nothing is going to stop you. You start at A and whatever happens you are determined to plough through to Z. There may be times when that is right, but please ensure that there is enough trust in the Lord to allow the Holy Spirit to whisper something to you. He may reveal to you that this cultist has a doubt over one aspect of the faith and that you should mention that subject. Don't think you can't, simply because this is not what you have prepared. The Lord may want to speak directly through you.

How will you hear or see these words? Probably not by someone writing them in the sky or by a booming voice in your ear. It will not be an audible voice at any level, but just a feeling within your spirit. Respond to that still, small voice as Elijah did. You will be nervous and there will probably be times when you make mistakes, but there will be other times when you see the Holy Spirit working. I remember spending several hours with two Jehovah's Witnesses and getting absolutely nowhere. It was about "I AM" and I was just about to go when I had a feeling that I should introduce a particular Scripture that I never usually mention to Witnesses. I will never forget the look on the face of one of them: it was just as if he had been hit in the stomach by a heavyweight boxing champion; I knew that at that point the Holy Spirit spoke to him.

We have looked at two hurdles in our preparation: knowing the truth of the Word of God, and knowing the life of the Holy Spirit, but there is still a further hurdle: knowing the way of prayer. Without prayer we will have little or no success in seeing cult members set free.

8 - Know the Way

> "And it came about that while He was praying
> in a certain place, after He finished, one of His
> disciples said to Him, 'Lord, teach us to pray,
> just as John taught his disciples.'"

From the incident that takes place at the beginning of Luke
11:1, we can draw two conclusions. First, one of the key
areas in discipleship is prayer. John had taught his disciples
to pray and now Jesus' disciples wanted Him to do the same.
Secondly, the way that Jesus prayed alerted the disciples to
the fact that they did not really know how to pray. Some of
these men had been with John and would have learned
something, but as they listened and watched Jesus, they knew
there was more that they should learn.

What is prayer?

First, prayer is not directed towards other people, but to God;
Matthew 6:5-6 makes this clear. We should not be trying to
use flowery language; in fact we should be using the most
practical language possible. Prayer is bringing our requests
and petitions to God, with genuine heartfelt words and an
expectation of His hearing and answering. Let us beware of
prayer that is written for people to hear and has no belief
behind it that the Lord will even listen, let alone answer.

Matthew 6:7 goes on to show that prayer does not come
from the mind but from the spirit. Prayer is something that
God inspires and not simply something which comes from
good man-made phrases. Luke 18:9-14 records the story of
the two men in the temple and it illustrates this point clearly.
The Pharisee, who it is said trusted in himself and told God
how great a man he was, received nothing. On the other hand,
the poorer man, who knew his true condition and cried from
his heart to God, received in abundance.

Matthew 6:7 does not put the emphasis just on the
repetition but on the meaningless repetition. We shall see

later that persistence, even using the same words, can be of God, but vain repetition week after week does not achieve anything. Words that come out of our own proud attitude are not received. God always resists the proud but gives grace and responds to the humble.

Probably one of the most helpful pictures of prayer is that of a circle. The Lord sits at the top of the circle and begins to express His will, and the circle begins to be drawn. We sit at the bottom of the circle and if we are listening for the voice of the Lord and respond, we will pray out from God's heart. The circle is then completed and returns fulfilled to God. Daniel is an example of this. He realised the will of God was for the people to go back to their land after the captivity and he knew the time was right. This did not mean that he just sat back and said: "That is fine. God has said it. He will do it." He completed the circle by praying three times a day until the thing was done. There will be people in the cults whom God wants to reach and He will remind us of them so we can pray for as long as necessary. Circumstances will be revealed to us and the Lord will show what He wants to do. We need to co-operate with Him and pray the matter to a conclusion. A similar picture is seen in Matthew 7:7: "… ask ... seek … knock". We first ask the Lord what is in His heart and He tells us. We then seek His will on the matter until we feel we are clear and we have found what He wants to do. Finally, we knock specifically on the door and the Lord will open the way to us. In all these things we are co-operating with God. He begins and we follow His will:

> "And this is the confidence we have before Him, that if we ask anything according to his will, He hears us. And if we know that He hears us *in* whatever we ask, we know that we have the requests which we have asked from Him." – 1 John 5:14-15.

Prayer is an adventure of listening to the Lord's voice and having the privilege of working with Him to see His will worked out on the earth.

Prayer makes the way

The answer that Jesus gave to the disciples in Luke 11 made it clear that one main purpose of prayer is to bring the kingdom of God to earth. We have nothing in ourselves of any lasting value to give to cult members. At the same time many of these people have been heavily influenced by satanic power and we cannot break this by ourselves. The only way that we are going to help them is by seeing God move in power, and prayer is the key to that.

I have been made aware of many pitfalls in this ministry and I believe we need to have a clear understanding of what the Lord teaches about prayer and how we should be praying. First, because prayer is making the way for the Lord, it should be going on regularly before meeting individuals. Many people in the cults will not want to pray with you because they will feel that you are talking to Satan. Do not be worried about this. And don't feel that you must go through the routine of praying during the meeting. Why cause these people more problems? We are trying to build bridges to them, not bang them over the head.

One visitor to our stand told me how his pastor had taught that you should not discuss Scriptures with these people when they call at the door. You must not talk – you must simply bind the spirits within them. So the next time the Jehovah's Witnesses called, he bound the theological spirits that were in them. But before he had finished praying they were half way down the street – nothing had been achieved. The Witnesses would now be convinced that all Christians were of the devil. We will need to pray strongly for them, but before they arrive and after they leave. If any prayer goes on while they are there it will normally be silent; God still hears!

If we look at Jesus' life we see how He handled this matter of prayer. He did not stop and pray before each sermon He gave or before each person was brought to Him for ministry. He had been praying the night before or in the early morning and He was ready to minister. It can just be superstition to want to start every meeting with prayer. If you have been praying beforehand you are ready to minister and praying in front of the cultist may simply be a hindrance.

A spiritual battle

We must never forget that we are in a battle with our spiritual enemy, not with the person we are talking to. Therefore the warfare should be undertaken in the spiritual realms and not with the people concerned. The condition of the cultists we are dealing with is aptly expressed by 2 Corinthians 4:4: "... the god of this world has blinded the minds ..." If we are to see them released, then the battle of the mind has to be won.

Pray constantly for the cult members in your area. Pray especially when you know people are coming, and pray for people you know by name. If they live next door, lay hands on the wall but do not walk round the house six times if it's semidetached (remember Jericho!). I remember a local prayer meeting a few years ago. The house at the bottom of the garden belonged to a Jehovah's Witness elder and the Lord gave us the desire to pray very strongly for him. The following Saturday I noticed some Witnesses in our road and, as they never knock at my door, I went out to mend the garden gate! A friendly "Good morning" stopped them in their tracks and before long we were sitting in my front room. After an hour or more of good conversation, I asked for the address to send them some more information. I nearly shouted "Hallelujah!" when one of them told me he lived in the very house we had been praying for. I still believe the Lord wants to work in that family.

We also need to pray that the battle already won in the heavenly places will be worked out on the earth. Pray that cult members will be open to receiving the truth of Scripture. If you feel inadequate for the battle be encouraged by the story of David and Goliath in 1 Samuel 17. David was the smallest and youngest in his house but God saw his heart.

The secret of David's victory was not what happened five minutes before he met Goliath but what had been going on in the fields with the sheep. David had learned to trust the Lord, and practised on the lion and the bear, which held no fear for him. They could not steal any sheep when the Lord was in control. This enemy was no different, and the same lessons of trust that he had learnt in the wilderness came into play here.

He refused Saul's armour that he had not tested, but instead trusted weapons that he had learned to use in the wilderness. The heat of the battle was no place for experimentation and so he used what he had tested and knew worked. He also knew he could sling the stone to land where he wanted it to, and the armour would only slow him down. He therefore went to the brook to get the stones because they needed to be smooth. What was real in his life, what he had learned to trust, was what he used in the battle with Goliath.

Be encouraged. Even if you feel you are the smallest and the least, God wants to teach you lessons now that you can use in His warfare later. Learn to trust Him where you are now and He will use you in greater ways in the days ahead. Learn to use things that are real to you and that have been tried and tested outside the heat of battle – putting on 'Saul's armour' could be a big mistake. David would have been hampered by something He did not know how to handle and would not have been able to run at Goliath as he did. Use what has been tested and is real to you.

'Binding and loosing'

There are many phrases that people use in prayer; 'binding and loosing' is one of the most common. There is nothing wrong with it unless we simply pick up these words and bandy them around without knowing what they mean. The only thing that sets free is truth, reality. If what we say is not based on truth or reality in our lives then it has no power. We must pray strong prayers to see these people set free but our prayers must be based on reality. It is vital that we are real ourselves and do not do anything simply because someone else does it. When using any method in prayer, we need to ask, 'Is it scriptural?' If the answer is no, then do not hesitate to discard it. If the answer is yes, then we need to ask, 'Is it right for me?' Only if it is real to me should I begin to use it.

The teaching of binding and loosing is usually taken from two places in Scripture. First, in Matthew 16:19, where Jesus is telling Peter the authority that the church has in Him. The original version of the New American Standard Bible translated this in what appears to be the most accurate way:

> "I will give you the keys of the kingdom of heaven; and whatever you shall bind on earth **shall have been** bound in heaven, and whatever you shall loose on earth **shall have been** loosed in heaven."

The emphasised words are not in later editions but hold the key understanding this verse. Is Jesus saying that whatever the church on earth decides to bind or loose then heaven will follow suit? This would put heaven and the Lord of heaven at the mercy of His people. Surely what it is saying is that first, the will of heaven is revealed on a matter concerning what shall be bound and what loosed. At this point the church then agrees with heaven and the matter is ratified. In other words, heaven moves first and then earth responds. It is interesting that Matthew uses these same words in chapter 18:18 about forgiveness and discipline within the church. I would not say that we cannot use these words in any other way, but that is the way they are applied here.

The other passage to mention is Mark 3:27. There is no way that we can plunder the property of Satan without Satan being bound. These are not just flippant words. The meaning of binding is to 'put under the obligation of the law'. In other words, there is a law at work that has to be obeyed even by Satan. What law can that be? The law that says that Jesus has already bound the strong man. He did it once and for all at

Calvary and we read in Ephesians 4:8 that He led captive a host of captives. We can declare today that Satan must release the captives because of what Jesus did two thousand years ago, not because we declare something today. This is the strong foundation that we can pray from; this is how we can plunder the goods. Learn how to pray strongly with others and to declare God's power to break Satan's hold because of the finished work of Jesus. Do not just mouth words but see the reality behind them. The fellowship I was brought up in used to call it 'executive' prayer. It was the signature at the bottom that ensured the document was carried out. Jesus has finished the work but He wants us to declare this in specific situations with specific people.

Prayer with fasting

Mark 9:14-29 relates how the Lord, after descending from the Mount of Transfiguration, was faced with a demonised boy. Try as they might the disciples could not help the lad and in the end (9:29) Jesus says that this sort will not come out except by prayer and fasting. This, at first sight, might appear to mean that the more we pray and fast the more demons we will see come out. However, I do not believe that this is the meaning of these verses. Demons come out by the command of the Lord and not simply by prayer and fasting. What I believe is that the prayer and fasting deepens and broadens our relationship with the Lord so we are ready to face such challenges. The more we know the Lord the more we are prepared to deal with these situations. Again, the prayer and fasting go on before the ministry takes place. This is the preparation ground that gives the Lord the insight and ability to deal with the demonised boy.

What we have seen, then, is that prayer is a vital preparation; a preparation both for us and for those to whom we minister. There is no substitute and prayer must be the key to a successful ministry in God's eyes.

Always Being Ready!

Prayer for deliverance

So far we have talked about the prayer that has gone on beforehand to prepare the way. Prayer for deliverance takes place with the person present. The cultists will have come to realise their need and will be willing to renounce their old way of life and receive Christ. This will not automatically mean that several demons have to be cast out of them. We should not try to bind the spirit of this or that just on the assumption that it must be there. In my experience there has not been the need to cast out spirits from many of those who have been in the cults, although usually some form of deliverance has been needed.

I believe that most cases of deliverance for the cultist are for the 'renewing of the mind' (Romans 12:2) and not for kicking out demons. A control has been placed over the mind as to what they receive and how they believe once information is given. This needs to be broken so that the person can receive the truth of God's Word and not read it through the filter given to them by the group they were in.

In some cases, though, there might be need for deliverance from demon activity too; for instance, some Mormons who have been involved with temple ceremonies for the dead, have been influenced by the demonic realm.

An illustration of this can be seen in the gospels. The woman taken in adultery (John 8) had no demons cast out of her. She received the Word of God that could be applied to her life and cause the necessary change – repentance and an acceptance of that Word into her life. However, we read of Mary Magdalene that she had seven demons cast out of her. We need to be aware of both possibilities as we help people in prayer and counselling. We must not jump to conclusions and try to cast out something that is not there; that only makes matters worse.

Unfortunately there is no A-Z of deliverance, but there are some main areas that we will probably need to cover.

First, we will talk about someone who does not need anything cast out of them.

A person has come to the realisation that the group they have been involved with is wrong and they need to confess this. They will not need to confess that the people are wrong, and they may still regard them as their friends. Their confession will be that they have been deceived into error and they want to own up to it now. Secondly, they will need to repent and turn their back on the teachings of the group. Testimony should be made that they want to be set free and that no longer will they associate with the beliefs and ethos of the group; they need to renounce the system they were involved in. James 4:4 tells us that if we are friends of these things not of God, we are God's enemy.

Once this has been done, we can pray for any influence that there has been over the person's life, to be broken in the name of the Lord. The captive can be set free because of the finished work of Jesus Christ. It might help the person you are praying with if they see that the blood and sacrifice of Jesus Christ are totally sufficient to forgive and deliver them from the past. Read such Scriptures such as Revelation 12:11, Ephesians 1:7, Romans 5:9, and Hebrews 13:12.

There are also Scriptures that show that it is important to confess specifically what they have been involved in so that the door can be closed completely. Revelation 2:4, 5 tells us that the Christians in Ephesus had to "remember from where they had fallen". We see this principle in Abraham's life too. After leaving God's will for his life and going down to Egypt, he had to return to the exact place he had left (Genesis 12:8-13:4). To return to God's will, he needed to realise where he had left it.

These first two steps bring a person from the influence of Satan to the influence of the kingdom of God. They first acknowledge to themselves and then confess to the Lord that they have been wrong. Their attitude shows that their repentance is true and a change can take place. But this is still not the end of the praying – it is just the beginning.

Always Being Ready!

We cannot leave them there because there would be a vacuum in their life. Now we need to pray and ask the Holy Spirit to come and fill every nook and cranny of the area that has been left empty. This is vital. In the Old Testament (Exodus 23:29-30) God said that he would not drive all the enemies out of the promised land at once, because the wild animals would take control. He was going to drive them out little by little and the children of Israel would be able to possess each part. As we drive the enemy out of any part of a person's life, the 'land' must come under the Lord's control.

Praying for those demonised

This cannot be a complete treatise on the subject, but you will probably meet the problem at some stage, and I believe we need to deal with it. Let me say first of all that, if you come face to face with a demonised person and you have fear about dealing with it, do not get involved. Back off and deal with the fear, and if necessary at that time, find someone else to whom you can pass them. Fear is Satan's biggest weapon. We should not allow him to win the victory for ever over it, but we must be realistic. When God was preparing the army for Gideon all those who were afraid were sent home (Judges 7:3). When Jehoshophat faced all the enemies we are told that he was afraid (2 Chronicles 20:3). However, he dealt with it by turning to seek the Lord. Be honest if there is fear in your life, but then seek the Lord Whose love casts out fear.

We should also add the warning, "Don't try this at home!" Do not just 'have a go' because you saw someone else do it. Ensure that there at least two of you and that you know the Lord is with you and working through you.

Secondly, we should note carefully the simplicity of Jesus dealing with demons in Luke 4:35, 8:32-33, and elsewhere. It may not be possible for us to be always as simple and efficient but we do not need to over-complicate matters. There is a school of thought around that seems to make deliverance a science that needs a PhD. Demons are categorised into many subsections and each must be dealt with differently. So much to learn and if you do it in the wrong order or in the wrong place, things might get worse. Don't be fooled into thinking that deliverance is only for the brainy. Human intelligence has little if anything to do with it; it is the Spirit Who teaches us and leads in this matter.

We may talk about 'oppression' or 'possession' but Scripture shows that it is being affected by Satan. The Greek word found in the four gospels is *damonzomai* which means 'demonisation,' that is – being affected by Satanic forces. As we have said, not everyone we deal with in the cults will be demonised and it may be relatively few, and so we need to pray that the Holy Spirit will help us discern the situation.

For instance, Luke 4:28 shows Satan using a temporary foothold; the people were enraged with Jesus, and Satan used that to get them to attack Him, but just because someone loses their temper from time to time does not mean that they have a 'spirit of rage'. It may be comforting to put the blame there but it is not true and no amount of 'deliverance' will solve the problem. To deal with temper we need to have a fresh understanding of what it means to be crucified with Christ. I remember seeing a well-known evangelist stomping on cigarette packets and binding the spirits of nicotine. I thought then, and still do think, that such an action is not based on Scripture. Many are hooked physically on nicotine as a drug. It is not the spirit of nicotine that needs to be driven out; rather it is the Lord who needs to come in and help them to exercise their will and deny themselves. But if we discern true demonisation, then the spirit must be cast out. There are a few occasions in Scripture when the spirit was commanded to leave the person without any co-operation on their part, but in practice, it is normal for there to be some co-operation on the part of the person. Usually this takes the form of repenting and turning their back on the practice that opened the doorway in the first place. I would add that I believe that it is dangerous to seek to perform deliverance without the person being willing to put their life under the Lord's sovereignty. How will anything actually change in the long term?

Always Being Ready!

Will not Satan simply return – because the doorway is still open – and so make things worse'?

Having come to the point of repentance, the demonic influence can be resisted in the name of the Lord. Once a person has stated that he wants to bring his life under the control of the Lord Jesus we can, as Scripture tells us, resist the devil. Then the doorway needs to be closed that had been open for Satan to come in and out just as he wanted, just as the children of Israel needed to close the door on their wanderings in the wilderness (Joshua 5:2-9). We need to make strong prayer and supplication for the grace and mercy of God to close that door now that repentance has come.

We have simply outlined the principles involved and I do not want to give the impression that it will be easy. There will be battles, but if we know our ground we can stand against the enemy. Take heart from Eleazer (1 Chronicles 11:12-14), one of David's mighty men, who stood firm in a barley field because it belonged to the Lord!

Persistence

Whichever way they have come, it is still just the beginning for the cultists who have been set free. Just as there was the need lay the foundation of basic doctrine, so there is the need to continue to pray for them. Pray that they will grow in God and in the knowledge of Him. Pray that they will learn to resist Satan and to stand for truth and reality in Christ. Pray that they will be established in the church and be used in the ministry to which God calls them.

We end this chapter with the remarkable parable in Luke 18:1-8. Here we find the widow woman who came every day to the judge, repeatedly saying the same thing. It was a plea from her heart and she did not bother finding different words; she was very specific and very practical in what she said. The Lord shows that if this unrighteous judge in the end gave in, how much more will our God in heaven respond to the cries of his people and bring righteous judgement to them. Let us not grow weary but continue to plead and intercede to the righteous judge to act and set these captives free, captives who have been bound by deception although they had sought for the truth. Will not our righteous Judge and heavenly Father hear our cries on their behalf?

Section 3

Overview of what Christians Believe

9 - What Do We Believe?

(1) God and the Bible

Often when I have been describing the belief of a cult, Christians have looked at me fairly blankly, either wondering what is wrong with such a belief, or knowing it's wrong, but having no idea how to answer it.

No self-respecting firm would ever send representatives out on the road without first giving them ample training about the company and products they represent. Most of us do not welcome door-to-door salesmen at the best of times, but one who doesn't know what he's talking about will certainly not be tolerated for long.

At election time the speeches we hear do not normally tell us what the candidate's party believes but more what the opposition does not. You even wonder if they spend more time looking at the manifesto of the opposition than their own.

These examples can teach us lessons in the Christian life. First, we need to know about the 'company' and 'product' we represent. There is no way we can help others if we cannot explain what we believe. Secondly, although we may talk about the 'opposition' we must also be able to say what we believe and why our 'party' is best. Apologetics are vital when we are speaking with anybody, but even more so with those in the cults, who feel they already have the truth. The word apologetics is derived from the Greek word *apologia* and means 'a reasoned argument', not to apologise. The word is used eight times in the New Testament; (Acts 22:1; 25:16; 1 Corinthians 9:3: 2 Corinthians 7:11; Philippians 1:7, 16; 2 Timothy 4:16; 1 Peter 3:15). It means 'a verbal defence, of what one has done or a truth in which one believes'. Again, the word 'defence' is not negative, but a very positive vindication, as the Scriptures above show. The only way we can do this is to know what we believe and then we can make a clear presentation of the facts.

For a more in depth look at apologetics see details of Reachout Trust's, *Should Christians Apologise*? in the Guide to Helpful Materials on p.210.

We are going to look at what the Scriptures teach on several subjects, in order to identify what is false. During our investigation we will also show how we can express to a cult member why we believe the Bible teaches what we claim it does.

God

The Bible never seeks to 'prove' God. Its opening words are that in the beginning God was there. The psalmist says that it is only the fool who says there is no God. Paul in Romans 1:19-20 shows that the evidence of God is all around us. His invisible attributes, eternal power and divine nature are clearly to be seen and there is therefore no excuse for not believing that He exists.

The God of Scripture is infinite. In the beginning He was already there, the only One to be truly eternal. We often think eternal means to have no end but in reality it means to have no beginning or end. God alone fits this description.

God is immutable; that is, He never changes. Hebrews 6:17-18 shows how we can totally rely on God because of His unchanging covenant.

Other attributes the Scriptures give to God are:

- Omnipresence – being everywhere (Psalm 139:7-10)

- Omnipotence – He is all-powerful. He spoke and the worlds came into being; He laughs at all that human beings can do (Psalm 2); He alone can stop human beings from doing what they plan to do (Genesis 11:6-9)

- Omniscient – the only One who has perfect knowledge.

Although this great God is the sovereign ruler of the universe, He still reveals Himself in a personal way. The 'I AM' (not the 'I was' or 'I will be') always reveals Himself to His people not as an impersonal force but as a loving Creator God (Hebrews 1:1-3). He is a loving God Who wants all of us to be saved and have an eternal future with Him.

So we can clearly see the difference between the God of the Bible and the impersonal force of the New Age and other religions.

Jesus Christ

Most cults will accept God; but most will attack the Person and deity of Christ. They will normally downgrade Jesus to being something less than God, and lift man up to His level. What does Scripture teach?

Is Jesus a created being?

Different groups will twist various scriptures to 'prove' that He is. We will look at one or two of these and see what they really teach.

Often the word firstborn is taken to mean 'first to be created'. Let's look for example at Colossians 1:15:

> "He is the image of the invisible God, the firstborn over all creation."

The word translated 'firstborn' is the Greek word *prototokos* and means the first-begotten. It can never mean the first one to be born. Its meaning is priority to or pre-eminence over; therefore Jesus is the pre-eminent One over all creation and not a created being Himself.

The problem arises because most translators use the English word 'firstborn' as it best describes the Greek. We need to discover what the Greek word actually means and how it was used at the time the New Testament was written.

Always Being Ready!

The word is also used in Colossians 1:18.

> "He is also head of the body, the church; and He is the beginning, the firstborn from the dead..."

Does it mean that Jesus was the first one to be born from the dead? That could not be true because in the New Testament there were at least three others before Jesus, including Lazarus, apart from those mentioned in the Old Testament. Is the Scripture wrong? It must be if Jesus is called the first one to be born from the dead. There is no confusion, however, when we take the true meaning of the Greek word as position, place or ranking. This is clearly seen in the Old Testament where, on at least two occasions, the first to be born lost the position of 'firstborn' to the second to be born. 'Firstborn' has always, in the Hebrew tradition, had to do with place and pre-eminence. The end of the above verse makes this abundantly clear:

> "... so that He Himself will come to have first place in everything."

Greek scholar W. E. Vine, in his *Expository Dictionary of New Testament Words*, points out that in Exodus 4:22 it was impossible for the whole of Israel to be the firstborn. It must be referring to their position and place before the Lord. Again, in Deuteronomy 21:16-17, a second-born son can become the firstborn by giving him the pre-eminence! We could also refer to Jeremiah 31:9 'Ephraim is my firstborn'. God has told a lie, because Ephraim was not the first to be born! The explanation is found in Genesis 48 where Israel blessed Ephraim and gave him the pre-eminence although he was not first to be born.

Did Christ have a pre-existence?

There are groups who say that Christ did not exist until He came to earth. However, John 1:1-5 clearly shows that Biblically this is not possible.

What Do We Believe?

John 1:1 literally means, "When the beginning begun Jesus was already there," He is an eternal Being and must have had an existence before coming to earth. Verse 3 also tells us that through Him *all* things came into being, and life was in Him. This cannot speak of an inanimate object but must speak of the person of Christ who existed before everything else.

Philippians 2:6-7 goes on to show that just as Jesus actually existed as man, He had already existed as God. Finally we can also mention John 8:58 that succinctly says that "before Abraham was, I AM." Jesus was in existence before Abraham and therefore clearly had a life before He came to earth.

What was declared at his birth?

Many cults teach that Jesus did not really become the Christ until His baptism, but the angel's message was quite clear:

> "For *today* in the city of David there has been born for you a Saviour, *who is* Christ the Lord"
> – Luke 2:11 (my italics).

Who does the Bible declare that Jesus is?

In John 5:16 we find Jesus being persecuted for healing on the Sabbath. His response to this begins: "My Father..." From this the Jews understood that Jesus was claiming to be equal with God.

This may seem straightforward and easily understood, but still some groups will try to wriggle round the scripture. They will use arguments such as that it was the unbelieving Jews who were calling Jesus God, and we should not believe what unbelieving Jews say! The answer to this argument comes in two stages.

First, Jesus had a way of saying the most profound things so that no one could understand Him, for instance, the parable of the sower in Matthew 13. But here He spoke plainly so that the people understood. Secondly, Jesus was a

Jew and understood how the Jewish mind worked. He knew that when he said, "My Father"; the Jews would understand that He was claiming to be of the same substance as God.

If Jesus is not equal with God, who has got it wrong – Jesus – or the Jews who believed what Jesus was saying? Of course in these circumstances Jesus would be at fault. This would make Him a liar and a fraud. He obviously is neither of these things and therefore the statement that He was claiming to be equal with God must be correct.

John 20:24-30 records the second time that Jesus appeared to the disciples, after His resurrection, but the first time that Thomas sees Him. Thomas's response was to acknowledge Jesus as, "My Lord and my God." Again this would seem fairly clear, but some groups will argue that it does not really mean what it says. Read the verse carefully. First, it clearly says that Thomas was speaking to Jesus. Secondly, the Greek here is emphatic; Thomas' words are *ho theos*, 'the God' – not just 'a god'. If this were not so, Jesus would have had to rebuke Thomas, but in verse 29 He commends all those who will believe the same as Thomas believed. In the midst of those who were to go out to teach the early church, Jesus accepts the acclamation that He was God. What did the apostles believe? They believed that Jesus was God. What must we believe from this incident? Clearly that Jesus knowingly and readily accepted the acclamation of being God.

In Revelation 5:13-14 we have an insight into Jesus' heavenly ministry. Who is receiving this honour, glory and worship? The One on the throne (The Father) and the Lamb (Jesus). Are we not to do what heaven is doing?

Every creature gives this glory to Jesus, Who therefore cannot be a created being. If Jesus is less than God, if He is really a created being, even a created heavenly being, the Bible would show that there was idol worship in heaven – creature worshipping creature. No angels, except fallen ones, no other heavenly creatures ever receive worship; only God receives worship in His heavenly kingdom. Jesus therefore must be God.

Summary

In summary we discover about Jesus:

1. Jesus is not created but eternal, always being in existence, without a beginning.

2. He was the Christ, the Messiah at birth.

3. He is declared to be God.

The Holy Spirit

In the fourth century there was a group known as the Pneumatomachians, literally, 'fighters against the Spirit'. Their attack was against the deity of the Holy Spirit. There are many cult groups today who continue this fight. Some will even take it further and deny not only His deity but His personality too. They will claim that He is not at work in this age and the gifts of the Holy Spirit must be satanically inspired.

In talking about the Holy Spirit to such groups we need to cover three areas:

1. Does the Bible show the Holy Spirit to be God?

2. Does the Bible show that the Holy Spirit has a personality?

3. What does the Bible have to say concerning the work of the Holy Spirit among Christians today?

We need to remember that this will not be just an intellectual battle, and we will not be just showing off our Biblical knowledge; we will be using scripture in such a way as to give the Holy Spirit Himself an opportunity to reveal the truth:

> "But a natural man does not accept the things of the Spirit of God; for they are foolishness to him, and he cannot understand them, because they are spiritually appraised" – 1 Corinthians 2:14.

Always Being Ready!

Does the Bible show the Holy Spirit to be God?

An unbiased reading of Scripture will show several references that prove beyond any reasonable doubt that the Holy Spirit is God. First, let's look at what Jesus said of the Holy Spirit:

> "And I will ask the Father, and He will give you another Helper, that He may be with you for ever" – John 14:16.

W. E. Vine in his *Expository Dictionary of New Testament Words* points out that the Greek word for 'another' in John 14:16, "denotes another of the same kind." This One Who was coming would be of the same kind as Jesus – not different. Just as Jesus was of the 'substance' of God, the Holy Spirit would be of the same kind.

The Bible reveals that the Holy Spirit is distinct from the Father and the Son (John 14:16 and Acts 2:33), but it also gives a simple and clear declaration that the Holy Spirit is God. In Acts 5:3 we find that Ananias is said to have lied to the Holy Spirit, but in the very next verse Peter says that Ananias lied to God. To Peter and all in the early church, the Holy Spirit was God.

The Holy Spirit in the New Testament is identified with Yahweh (Jehovah) of the Old Testament. See, for example, Hebrews 3:7-11 where the Holy Spirit tells us that He was provoked and tested. As a result He said, "They shall not enter my rest." This passage in Hebrews is quoting from Psalm 95:7-11, and if you refer back to those verses you will find the psalmist is speaking of God. And further back still, where the incident is originally recorded in Numbers 14:23-30, we see that it is the "Lord Jehovah" who is speaking. The Holy Spirit is called by this name reserved for God. Scripture is not out to confuse us, and if it interchanges the Holy Spirit and God it is to show us that the Holy Spirit is God.

Divine works that God alone can accomplish are shown to be the work of the Holy Spirit. For instance, the work of creation is attributed to the Holy Spirit in Job 33:4 and Psalm 104:25-30, but Isaiah 44:24 and 45:18 show this is solely God's work. Also regeneration (John 3:5-6 and Titus 3:5) and the very important work of sanctification (Romans 15:16; 1 Corinthians 6:11; 2 Thessalonians 2:13 and 1 Peter 1:12).

Scripture gives further evidence of the deity of the Holy Spirit by showing He has attributes only found within God. He is eternal (Hebrews 9:14); omnipresent (Psalm 139:7-10); omnipotent (Luke 1:35; Romans 15:13-19 and 1 Corinthians 12:7-11); and omniscient (1 Corinthians 2:10-11 and Isaiah 40:13-14).

Note, too, the way that Scripture puts the Name of the Holy Spirit along with the Name of the Father and the Name of the Son. Two examples of this are found in the apostolic commission (Matthew 28:19-20) and the benediction in 2 Corinthians. A further significant piece of evidence is that the apostles recognised the sovereignty or lordship of the Spirit. Paul writes:

> "But whenever a man turns to the Lord, the veil is taken away. Now the Lord is the Spirit; and where the Spirit of the Lord is, there is liberty. But we all, with unveiled face beholding as in a mirror the glory of the Lord, are being transformed into the same image from glory to glory, just as from the Lord, the Spirit." – 2 Corinthians 3:16-18.

We will add one final point here by quoting from E. H. Bancroft:

> "The Holy Spirit can be blasphemed, and this is possible only of God. As spirit is nothing less than the innermost principle of life, and the spirit of man is man himself, so the Spirit of God must be God Himself (1 Cor 2:11). Thus the Scriptures teach that the Holy Spirit is a person having all the divine attributes and able to do all divine works." – *Christian Theology*, p.160.

Always Being Ready!

Does the Bible show that the Holy Spirit has a personality?

Clearly the Bible shows that the Holy Spirit is a power (see for instance, Luke 1:35), but I believe it also gives conclusive evidence of His personality.

Jesus Christ is called the Advocate in 1 John 2:1. The same Greek word translated *Comforter*, is used of the Holy Spirit in John 14:16. An impersonal force could not fulfil the function described here. The Holy Spirit is to be the *Paraclete*, meaning Someone who goes to court to speak for you – not a job for an impersonal force!

Another indication that the Scripture gives of the personality of the Holy Spirit is found in John 16:7-15. Here Jesus uses the masculine 'He' of the Holy Spirit twelve times although the noun translated 'spirit' is neuter. If these verses were to be grammatically correct they would have been written with the Holy Spirit being called 'it'. The fact that 'He' is used is a deliberate indication of the personality of the Holy Spirit.

> "But I tell you the truth, it is to your advantage that I go away; for if I do not go away, the Helper shall not come to you; but if go. I will send *Him* to you. And *He*, when *He* comes, will convict the world concerning sin, and righteousness, and judgement... But when *He* the Spirit of truth, comes, *He* will guide you into all truth; for *He* will not speak on *His* own initiative, but whatever *He* hears, *He* will speak; and *He* will disclose to you what is to come. *He* shall glorify Me; for *He* shall take of Mine, and shall disclose it to you. All things that the Father has are Mine; therefore I said, that *He* takes of Mine and will disclose it to you." – John 16:7-8, 13-15, (italics added).

What Do We Believe?

Personality is not just dependent on outward form and actions but on the life within. There are three areas that need to be present for someone to be classed as a person: intellect, will, and emotion.

First, let us look at what the Scriptures show concerning the Holy Spirit and an intellect. John 14:26 tells us that the Holy Spirit can teach and this is a sign of intellect. Romans 8:26-27 shows us that the Holy Spirit intercedes for us: again, a sign of intellect. Greek scholar W. E. Vine's definition of 'intercession' shows that an impersonal force could not do it:

> "Primarily to fall in with, meet with in order to converse; then to make petition, especially to make intercession, plead with a person, either for or against others." – *Expository Dictionary of New Testament Words*, Vol. 2, p. 267.

1 Corinthians 2:10-11 also tells us that the Holy Spirit can know the thoughts of God. A third clear sign that the Holy Spirit has an intellect.

Second, what do the Scriptures show concerning the Holy Spirit and a will?

Acts 8:29, 39, among other Scriptures, (see also Acts 10:19-20 and 16:6-7) show the Holy Spirit's work in directing the early church. Here He directs Philip in his ministry, a clear sign that the Holy Spirit has a will.

1 Corinthians 12:11 is clear that the Holy Spirit has a will of His own and can make decisions. He distributes the gifts just as He wills. W. E. Vine tells us the Greek word used here means:

> "To wish, to will deliberately . . . the deliberate exercise of the will." - *Expository Dictionary of New Testament Words*, Vol. 1. p. 299.

Again, we must conclude beyond all reasonable doubt that the Holy Spirit has a will.

Always Being Ready!

Third and finally, we need to see what the Scriptures show concerning the Holy Spirit and emotions.

We see that the Holy Spirit can love, Romans 15:30 and can comfort, Acts 9:31, both attributes that come from the heart and show emotion.

Ephesians 4:30 says that the Holy Spirit can be grieved. We again turn to W. E. Vine for the meaning of the Greek word used. It "denotes to cause pain, or grief, to distress, grieve." (*Expository Dictionary of New Testament Words*, Vol. 2, p. 178).

According to the Bible, the Holy Spirit possesses an intellect, a will and emotions, and can therefore be shown to be a person.

What does the Bible have to say concerning the work of the Holy Spirit among Christians today?

We already touched upon this in Chapter 7 when we were looking at the work of the Holy Spirit for today. Most will accept that 'holy spirit' as an impersonal force can be an extension of the power of God and can help us to one degree or another. Many will also accept that the fruit of the Spirit is necessary for our lives today. Can we then divorce this work of the Holy Spirit from His gifts which He distributes as He wills? Some cults will say that the gifts of the Holy Spirit are not for today. They were only necessary to see the early church established or until that which is perfect – the Bible – came into being. This last thought comes from 1 Corinthians 13:10 that says that when that which is perfect comes, the gifts that are partial will cease. However, what is 'that which is perfect', and has it come? As great as the Bible is, I do not believe it is 'that which is perfect' because it looks forward to something more: God setting up His kingdom. When we see the Lord face to face we will not need the gifts, but until then they reveal God to people and we should be seeking Him to release them through us for the ministry to the cults, among other things.

The work of the Holy Spirit in giving gifts is vital to bring in fullness and completeness, and I do not believe we can divorce this aspect of His work from others that Scripture shows He is doing. Let us then summarise the way the Bible shows that the Holy Spirit is working in the church today.

The church came into being via the Holy Spirit (Acts 2:1-4), and He alone is the One who can bring unity (1 Corinthians 12:12-27 and Ephesians 4:1-6).

He is the One who confers gifts and graces upon God's children to fulfil the work of the Lord (Romans 12:6-8, 1 Corinthians 12:4-11, Galatians 5:22-26, and Ephesians 4:8-13).

The Holy Spirit is the One who teaches Christians and the One Who directs the church in its outreach to the world (John 14:26, 1 John 2:20, 27, Acts 13:1-3, 16:7 and 20:28).

All aspects of the life of the church – preaching, prayer, etc – are dependent on the work of the Holy Spirit (Acts 10:44, 1 Corinthians 2:1-5, Romans 8:26-27, and Ephesians 5:18-19).

If the Third Person of the Trinity, the Holy Spirit, ceased His work on earth today there would be no Christian work. Sadly, the cults are not moving under the Holy Spirit and that is why they are not fulfilling a Christian ministry and do not even want to admit His work exists.

Lovingly we need to present to them the necessity for knowing the work of the Holy Spirit today, and to show that He needs to be at work in their own lives and in the life of the group to which they belong.

Summary

In summary, we discover about the Holy Spirit:

1. He is declared to be God.

2. He has personality and is not just a force.

3. He is still at work in the Church today.

The Trinity

Whereas it is not essential for someone to believe in the Trinity to be saved, I know that from personal experience, some groups will hardly talk to you unless you explain why you believe it. However, never try to prove the existence of the Trinity purely from a logical point of view. It is impossible. The Trinity is not logical to the human mind. We believe the Trinity with our hearts. We can explain that the chemical formula H_2O can be found as ice, water or steam. That certainly shows the idea behind the Trinity but it does not prove the Trinity exists. What we need to be able to show to the religious cults who spend their life denying the existence of the Trinity, is that the Bible reveals it. Whether we can accept it logically is irrelevant if the revelation of the Word of God is plain for us to see.

To most cult groups the Trinity is a problem and when the subject comes up many appear to lose interest. To groups such as the Jehovah's Witnesses, if you mention the word you are seen as part of the apostate church. They will make much of the fact that it is a pagan doctrine. They have even produced a colour booklet, *Should You Believe in the Trinity?* which clearly shows that they are right! They delight in giving this to churchgoers to confuse them.

Should we avoid the subject then? Not if we understand our own doctrine of the Trinity. Without understanding these things ourselves, there is little hope of expressing these truths to the sceptical, in a convincing way.

What follows is not a full treatise on the Trinity; there are other books that have undertaken that. What I want to do is to show that the Scriptures answer the main arguments put forward by the cults.

The Trinity is beyond reason

The religious cults that we are speaking to will all believe in God and the revelation of Him as they see it in the Bible. But

What Do We Believe?

God Himself is beyond human reason. Speaking to bring the world into being is not something we can reason out. The fact that God is everywhere, always, and can listen and speak to everyone is beyond reason. If, therefore, God is beyond human reason it is not surprising that doctrines concerning God also defy reason. We do not, and indeed cannot, fully comprehend God with our minds; we need to use our spirits too. Certainly the Trinity is beyond reason, but it is not beyond revelation. Just as we do not reject God because we cannot reason Him out, we should not reject the Trinity because it is beyond our mental capacity to understand it.

Further study can be undertaken with such Scriptures as Isaiah 55:11, John 1:14,16; 13-15, 1 Corinthians 2:9, 10, l4 and 2 Corinthians 3:5-18.

The sum of all its parts

Good defence lawyers will always seek to fragment the evidence brought against their client. They will try to isolate certain aspects of the testimony and show the weakness of it. The prosecution will seek to show that the strength of their case is that all the parts fit together and lead to one conclusion beyond any reasonable doubt.

Jehovah's Witnesses, among other cult members, delight in telling people that the word 'Trinity' is not found in the Bible. That is correct, but then the word Bible is not found in the Bible! The word was only coined to describe certain aspects of the Godhead and Their relationship to each other. There are even some clues to the Trinity in the Old Testament. Deuteronomy 6:4 tells us that there is One true God, with 'One' being a composite, not singular. There are also clues showing that God is more than one Person. See, for instance, Isaiah 48:16 and 63:9-10. However, if the Old Testament has the doctrine in shadow form, the New Testament clearly defines what we mean by the word 'Trinity'.

There are three distinct persons. Scriptures such as Matthew 28:19 and 1 Corinthians 12:4-6 describe the Three.

We can also see from John 5:37 that Jesus distinguishes Himself from the Father. Then in John 14:16, the Holy Spirit is called 'Another', distinguishing Him from both Father and Son.

Then Father is God. This is not usually disputed and we have already looked at this aspect.

Jesus is God. Again we have already dealt with this and verses such as John 5:21, 20:28 and Hebrews 1:3 clearly show it to be true.

The Holy Spirit is God. Many verses including Acts 5:3-4 and 2 Corinthians 3:16-18 show the truth of this statement.

All these specific aspects of the Trinity are clearly shown to be true according to the Word of God. The word 'Trinity' may not appear in the Bible but the Bible clearly teaches the idea of the Trinity in all its aspects.

The Bible

Can we rely on the Bible? We would answer a resounding 'Yes!' Can we then rely on the Bible more than any other 'religious' book? Again we would answer 'Yes' and would present the following evidence. *The Koran, The Book of Mormon*, or *Science and Health with Key to the Scriptures* or any other perceived book of Scriptures, cannot pass all the following tests as the Bible can.

The composition

No other book has been written by such a variety of human authors, living in such separated parts of the world over a time span of hundreds of years. Not only do we have the human impossibility of getting all the writings together, but when they are brought into one place, they miraculously fit to a divine pattern. The composition of the Bible clearly shows the hand of an eternal God, not the work of a human committee.

What Do We Believe?

The content

Nothing proves the Bible more than the test of time. The Bible talks about 'the circle of the earth' when everyone in those days thought the world was flat. Abraham was told about the millions of stars when comparatively few were visible. The Bible talked about 'this great city of Babylon' when it did not seem even to exist. Astronomy, archaeology, cosmology, geology and other sciences have all clearly proved statements in the Bible instead of showing them to be lies.

The prophecy

At least 700 years before it happened, the Bible foretold where Jesus would be born, how He would be born, why He would be born, and what would happen to Him through His life. No one could have made that up. And it needed the intervention of an eternal God to bring it all to pass.

The experience

No book has the power to change lives as the Bible does with its message of Calvary and Pentecost. Many other 'religious' books have passed away, but the Lord has watched over His Word. He has said that heaven and earth - and therefore all other books - will pass away before the Bible does.

The Bible can be trusted totally and relied upon completely. Scripture, as the Word of God, is 'breathed out' and inspired by the Holy Spirit. The men who penned the Words were not perfect – the Bible makes that abundantly clear – but the Words inspired by the Holy Spirit are perfect. They are there to make us complete, equipped for everything and lacking nothing (2 Timothy 3:17).

10 - What Do We Believe?

(2) Salvation

God makes it clear that there is nothing that we can do to deserve His salvation or to earn it. The moment we try to walk along the path of works, we are outside God's revelation. However, we do need to co-operate with God and accept what He has done, in order to receive salvation. Salvation is a finished work; nothing can be added to it. When Jesus said, "It is finished," He meant it. Humanity had become separated from God and the only way back was by blood sacrifice. The continual sacrifice of bulls and goats could only be temporary. The Book of Hebrews shows us that the permanent solution was the sacrifice, once and for all, by Jesus Christ.

Indeed, this is what makes Christianity different from every other belief system - every other belief system has a book and/or prophet that you must obey and as you do this you progress along the path and one day you hope to pass the finishing line. But Christianity begins at the end and we spend our lives working out what we have already received. This is the only sure way to salvation and, indeed, why Jesus said that He is the only way.

Ephesians 2 shows us just how He is the only way. Verse 1 tells us, "You are dead ..." Nothing we can do, no way we can respond, absolutely not one thing any of us can do in that state. It is not until, "(God) made us alive ..." (verse 5) that we can even respond to His grace and mercy. There is no room for works here.

From our side, how do we need to co-operate with God to receive salvation? There must be repentance, the voluntary change of mind of a sinner turning away from sin, an act of the will. We do not have the power to change our lives, but by applying our will to turn away from the past we show God our desire to receive salvation. Repentance, as it were, empties out the old and makes room for the new to be received. As John 1:12 says, "As many as received Him to them He gave the right to become children of God." We need then positively to receive Christ into our lives to fulfil His work in us. Salvation has nothing to do with us; it is the gift of God that must be received by faith based on what God has said (Ephesians 2:8-10). There are no works that we can do to receive salvation.

At this point we are justified. It is vitally important that we understand what that means; otherwise we will be grovelling around in the mire instead of standing on the rock. Justification means that God has declared us righteous and treats us as such. It has nothing to do with what we are as individuals, nor what we have accomplished; it is an act of declaration by God. Our place is to realise what God has done and live in the good of it. You could never in a thousand lifetimes, never in a million hours of prayer, bring yourself to righteousness. But God has pronounced it and He treats us as righteous. That is the place we start from.

The prodigal son is a great example of justification. Returning from the pigsty and from wasting his inheritance he found himself clothed immediately with the robe of righteousness (Luke 15:22). However, you would not expect the son to stay as he was underneath, full of dirt and grime. You would expect ongoing changes that would show his responsibility in the house. For a start, you would expect him to have a bath! And that is the process of sanctification. Justification is a once and for all act as Romans 5:1 shows, "having been justified". Sanctification is an ongoing process, "… resulting in sanctification' (Romans 6:19). We are being continually changed into His likeness.

Salvation by works or faith?

Most cults have the view that, works, to one degree or another, are *vital* to salvation. We want to emphasise the word *vital* because we believe that works do have their place and Christians should not just be pew-warmers and sermon-fodder. Can we, however, be saved without the use of works? Is it possible to come into a true relationship with Jesus Christ and know the forgiveness of sins without doing certain works?

Many groups will have quite complicated arguments and a well developed 'theology' to show their belief from Scripture. Simply put, though, what they are saying is that there is no way that we can be saved without some action on our part. Just responding to what Jesus said and receiving the benefits of what He has already accomplished is not enough.

The type of work needing to be accomplished will be slightly different depending on the group you are dealing with. Some groups will claim that you must join their group to be saved, even going as far as to say that there is no salvation outside their group. You certainly need Jesus but you also need to make a human commitment to an earthly group and work with them. Leave the confines of the group and you will leave your salvation behind.

There will be others who will claim that salvation can only come when the individual has accurate knowledge. The Watchtower Society has even translated the word 'know' in John 17:3 to prove this: eternal life is equated to 'taking in knowledge'. Our mental capacity becomes essential to being saved. This, of course, will immediately give the intelligent an unfair advantage and may mean that some can never be saved because of their lack of understanding. Is our God unfair and partial to rule out some people from salvation?

Still others will say that you must believe in the writings of a particular person who alone can lead you to the clear truth of salvation. Doing what they say is vital to salvation and those who do not follow them will never be saved.

Whatever slight variations there may be, the Scriptures show a different picture. We will look together at the teaching of the Bible on faith and works, and see what the relationship is. We must know what is essential for our salvation and what place works have in our relationship with God. If we are not clear on this, we will never be able to help those who are striving through works to reach God.

Should I rely on a person?

There are many within the cults who have been told that they must put all their trust in one person as this act alone will lead them to salvation. We have already looked at the subject of authoritarianism in Chapter 3 but we shall look at a couple of Scriptures here.

First, we are taught that we are never to put our trust solely in a created man or woman, no matter how great he or she is. The Psalmist declared, "It is better to take refuge in the Lord than trust in man. It is better to take refuge in the Lord than to trust in princes"(Psalm 118:8-9). Faith is to be placed in God alone (Mark 11:22). He alone cannot be moved.

Of course God has given us our brothers and sisters for strength and help, but not to rely on them instead of relying on God. True leadership will always point us to rely on the Lord and not encourage us to be dependent on another human being. If a man or woman becomes the centre of our faith and trust, there is something very wrong.

Another thing that we need to be clear about is that, nowhere in the New Testament, do we see someone working for an organisation to find God. Today, there are groups who give the impression that when you leave them you leave behind your salvation. What causes someone to be saved? The work of the Holy Spirit within the life. Can, then, the outward act of leaving a particular group cause me to lose my salvation? Such a teaching has no foundation in logic, let alone in Scripture. Some group members will need help to understand exactly what they do believe because their leaders may have confused them into accepting two opposites: salvation by faith and by works! A conversation to help them see the truth could go something like this:

CHRISTIAN: Would you say that you are saved by faith or by works?

CULT MEMBER: Definitely by faith.

CHRISTIAN: You believe then that your salvation is based on a relationship with Jesus Christ alone?

CULT MEMBER: Yes.

CHRISTIAN: Just suppose that you left your group tomorrow and unfortunately died the week after. Is your salvation secure?

CULT MEMBER: No, we can never be presumptuous; we have to stay loyal to God's people here on earth.

CHRISTIAN: But only your outward state has changed. You still have the same faith within.

CULT MEMBER: That does not matter; I would have left the group that God is using.

CHRISTIAN: Then your faith is in the outward belonging to the group and not the inward relationship with God.

CULT MEMBER: Well …

Faith is not of human origin

While talking to a cult member, it will probably not be necessary to give a full theological explanation of faith. It will certainly help, though, if you point out one or two things. The first statement you could make is that faith is not of human origin. This means that, when I say that I am saved by faith, it cannot mean that I am saved by works: the two are opposites.

Romans 10:17 shows that faith comes from receiving the Word of Christ. Naturally we do not have faith to tell a mountain to go into the sea (Matthew 17:20). Any natural 'faith' we have could not survive the testing by fire mentioned in 1 Peter 1:7. True faith that we have comes from

God, is increased by God and is tested by God. It is not positive thinking, mind over matter, or anything else that we try to do.

Faith is also shown to be interlinked with our relationship with the Lord, not an organisation. Galatians 2:20 reveals that Paul lived his new life by God's faith. How did he come to that place? Through knowing the reality of what it meant to be crucified with Christ. At that point he no longer lived by his own strength and motivation; now it was Christ's. Faith in Paul's life was clearly because of a relationship with Jesus Christ not the organisation that he had been involved in before.

Luke 17:5 records the request of the apostles to increase their faith, and the Lord's answer is very revealing. He tells the parable of the servant working all day in the field and then still having to come in and prepare his master's food and wait on him. The slave will not receive any special commendation because that is his relationship with the master. How did the Lord tell them to increase their faith? Should they join a particular group? Should they listen to the teaching of a particular man? No, they should ensure that their relationship with their Master is right. They should ensure that they are being obedient to all that He has said and then their faith will be increased.

Opportunity missed

The story of Mary and Martha recorded in Luke 10:38-42 is an excellent example of works in the New Testament. Jesus was invited into the home of Mary and Martha. Mary took the opportunity to sit at the Lord's feet and listen to His words. Martha, on the other hand, was flapping around doing many things, most of which were probably legitimate. However, whether the works were good or bad is not the point: they did not bring her closer to the Lord. On that day Martha should have dropped her works and taken the opportunity to receive the Lord and His words.

What Do We Believe?

The end of the story and the effect it had can be found in John 12:3. In the crowded room all the spectators were receiving from Jesus but few gave thought as to His needs. It was Mary who was then ready to give to the Lord. She knew in her spirit what He needed and was prepared to do the work. She had been prepared and received faith from sitting at the Lord's feet and now she could get involved with the works. We will see in a moment other Scriptures that show that this is the correct order.

Does eternal life come from working?

We need to ask this question because some groups will specifically say that they can work for the reward of eternal life. It is simply saying that works are essential for salvation in a different way. However, there are some clear Scriptural passages that we can look at that show it is impossible to receive eternal life as wages for our works.

Luke 10:25-28 and 18:18-23 record very similar stories. In both cases the question was asked, "What can I do to inherit eternal life?" Jesus answers both enquirers in a similar way. The lawyer in Luke 10 immediately tells Jesus what is written in the law: "You shall love the Lord your God ..." You are correct, replies Jesus, go and do that and you will have eternal life. Do what? Ensure that your relationship is right with the Lord. Eternal life is not a reward for doing anything; it is given freely to those who place a relationship with God at the centre of their lives.

The rich young ruler in Luke 18 comes to the same place via a slightly different route. Jesus tells him all the commandments of how to act towards men – in other words what works he should be manifesting. I've done all that, replies the ruler. Interestingly Jesus does not deny this but simply adds one other thing that he has not done. Now he needs to put aside the possessions that were in the centre of his life to ensure that God was at the centre. Again, eternal life does not come from doing works on earth but having a right relationship with God in heaven.

Always Being Ready!

We mentioned earlier those who feel knowledge is important for salvation. John 5:39 shows beyond any question that eternal life cannot come from taking in knowledge – it comes from Jesus.

Why then does the Bible mention works?

This is a very fair question because, if we should not be doing works, why does the Bible confuse us by mentioning them? We need to be clear; it is not that we should not be doing works but that we must get them in their right place. There is no way we can be saved and receive eternal life by works but, once saved, there are works for us to do.

Philippians 2:12 is very helpful here, reminding us that we are to work *out* our salvation, not work *towards* it.

Whenever you talk about works and faith with a cult member, it is almost inevitable that they will mention James 2:22. It is necessary, therefore, that we understand what is being said here. James begins the chapter by saying, "My brethren, do not hold your faith ..." So it becomes apparent immediately that he was writing to 'the brethren', those who had already received Christ and already had faith. What he goes on to show is that to have faith that is not expressed by works is useless.

> "Faith necessarily leads to good works... faith which does not lead men to act upon commands and promises of Christ – or, in other words, does not lead to obedience, is called in Scripture a 'dead,' that is, an unreal faith." – E. H. Bancroft, *Christian Theology*, p. 253.

James 2:22 shows that works *perfect* our faith. There is no point in claiming that we have faith if we do not show it. Works express what faith is already; they do not create faith. This whole subject is best summed up in Ephesians 2:8-10:

> "For by grace you have been saved through faith; and that not of yourselves, it is the gift of God; not as a result of works, that no one should boast. For we are His workmanship, created in Christ Jesus for good works, which God prepared beforehand, that we should walk in them."

The order is highlighted by these verses. Works can do nothing to enable us to receive salvation. It is God's gift alone and all we can do is get down on our knees and receive gratefully and humbly what He is offering to us. However, once we are saved, there are works prepared for us to do. We are not working *towards* our salvation but working *out* our salvation. This is the biblical picture of works and faith.

Is baptism essential for salvation?

Many cults will say that to be saved you must be baptised. Some will even go as far as to say that unless you are baptised in our church you are not saved. Is this what Scripture teaches or is this a clear sign of 'another' gospel? We are not asking if baptism is an important act; there is no doubt in my mind that Scripture commands us to be baptised by immersion as believers, but that is not the subject in question. What we need to answer is: Does the Bible show that baptism is essential for salvation? In other words is there any way that I can know the saving work of Jesus Christ in my life if I am not baptised? Alternatively, if, as we say baptism is an important act, does it follow salvation? Also, does it give a clear testimony to both those on earth and the principalities and powers of what has already happened?

The groups that teach that baptism is essential for salvation will normally use several verses to prove this doctrine from Scripture. These are the ones we need to look at and understand. We can then talk to the cult member and show them that maybe the scriptures they thought proved one thing actually teach another.

Always Being Ready!

There are also some verses in the Bible that give a positive declaration of salvation without baptism and some groups admit that there are problems in explaining them. These, therefore, are often good to use at the beginning to introduce the subject.

Luke 23:42-43 records the repentance of the thief on the cross. He is told that he will be with the Lord that day and yet he never received baptism. Baptism was certainly not essential to the salvation of that man. This also highlights the teaching of Jesus concerning salvation and baptism. He was baptised under John's baptism but He did not teach that if anyone was to be saved they must be baptised. We have declarations such as John 3:16, where a clear promise of salvation and deliverance is made providing there is an acting on what the person has heard. No mention is made at all of baptism and yet the Word of God says this person will not perish but have everlasting life.

We can see a similar incident in Romans 10:9-10, 13. Here Paul, under the inspiration of the Holy Spirit, says that if we call on the Lord we will be saved. If we confess with our mouth and believe in our heart we shall be saved. This is God's word and cannot be added to or subtracted from and it gives a clear promise of salvation without baptism.

This same situation is found in 1 Corinthians 15:1-5 where Paul makes known the essentials of the gospel. These were the things that were of first importance. In a chapter where he was going to use an illustration of those who baptised for the dead, I am sure he would have not left out baptism if it was essential. However, the definition is all about the person of Christ and not about baptism. Christ died, He was buried, He rose again and He appeared. This is the gospel, centred in the person and the work of Jesus Christ, not what I do.

Such a presentation should lay the foundation for talking about verses in Scripture that may appear to show that baptism is essential for salvation.

What Do We Believe?

> "And Peter said to them, 'Repent, and let each of you be baptized in the name of Jesus Christ for the forgiveness of your sins; and you shall receive the gift of the Holy Spirit.'" – Acts 2:38.

If this verse is taken out of context it could possibly mean that you need to be baptised to be saved. Initially it does link 'remission of sins' with both repentance and baptism. However, we need to know what the phrase 'for the remission of sins' actually means. Does it mean 'in order to', because then the verse would clearly show that baptism was essential if we want our sins forgiven?

The Greek word translated 'for' is *eis* and it is used some 1,488 times in the New Testament. In all these hundreds of times it is never translated 'in order to'. Young's *Concise Critical Bible Commentary* renders it literally, 'with a view to a letting go of sins'. If Peter does not mean to say that baptism was essential to be saved, just what was he meaning to say? Peter was talking to Jews in whose mind actions always followed faith. In such a context it would be natural, therefore, for Peter to talk about the action as well as the faith. However, what is also very instructive is to note that on other occasions, for instance Acts 2:21 and 3:19, he did not mention baptism. Does it mean that what Peter said on those occasions was not the true gospel and the people who acted on his words were not saved? That cannot be true but what is seen is that there are times when baptism is mentioned and there are times when it is not.

The common factors, which are always mentioned, are the repenting and calling on the Lord. These are shown to be the essentials of the gospel. We must always consider the whole of Scripture and does that mean that John 3:16 and Ephesians 2:8-10 along with the other Scriptures mentioned are only half truths? No, God does not make such mistakes. He ensures that the essential elements of the gospel are always preached.

Verses that teach baptism is essential for salvation?

Romans 6:3-4

> "Or do you not know that all of us who have been baptized into Christ Jesus have been baptized into His death? Therefore we have been buried with Him through baptism into death, in order that as Christ was raised from the dead through the glory of the Father, so we too might walk in newness of life."

There are several baptisms mentioned in the Scriptures, and each has three elements.

1. The person doing the baptising.

2. The person being baptised.

3. The medium into which they are baptised.

Romans 6 is not talking about a literal baptism into water, but being 'baptised into Christ'. These verses are not talking about an outward act that takes place in water but rather an inward act that takes place when you receive Jesus Christ. When you look carefully at these verses, you will see that they actually prove that water baptism is not essential for salvation. Paul was talking about an inward experience - not an outward one - that brought these people to new birth and new resurrection life.

1 Peter 3:21

> "And corresponding to that, baptism now saves you – not the removal of dirt from the flesh, but an appeal to God for a good con-science through the resurrection of Jesus Christ."

What Do We Believe?

This Scripture, at first glance, may appear to say that baptism now saves you, but note in the previous verses to what it is corresponding. Baptism saving you corresponds to the flood. We need to discover three things: what actually saved the people from the flood; what was the salvation from; and what was it to.

If this was to teach us that New Testament baptism saves, then we would need to see that it was the water that saved Noah and his family. However, the water did not save them; rather the opposite – it nearly destroyed them. What actually saved them was the ark. We need to discover in New Testament terms what or whom the Old Testament picture of the ark represents, and the answer is *not* baptism but Jesus Christ. Being put into water does not save us; our safety comes from being in Christ and having a sure relationship with Him.

What sort of salvation was this? Are we talking about the salvation of receiving Christ into the life? No, in Old Testament terms, they needed that relationship *before* they got into the ark. This was a salvation that would take them *out* of one world system *into* another. Salvation is not being used here in the sense of being born again. It is a full deliverance, through God's judgement, into the new world order that Christ has yet to set up on earth.

Mark 16:16

> "He who has believed and been baptized shall be saved; but he who has disbelieved shall be condemned."

Note in this verse that condemnation does not come because of lack of baptism, but because of not believing. There is no evidence from this verse to show that baptism is essential for salvation but it does show that believing is essential. This verse also needs to be compared with Matthew 28:19. Here the disciples – those who had already repented and entered Christ's school – are then baptised.

Always Being Ready!

Acts 22:16

> "And now why do you delay? Arise, and be
> baptized, and wash away your sins, calling on
> His name."

Again this verse seems to say that when Paul was baptised, he washed his sins away. Does this fit in with the evidence that we have concerning Paul's conversion? If the Scripture shows that Paul was already converted at his baptism, it would mean that it was an outward act signifying what had already happened within.

In Acts 22:8 Paul called Jesus 'Lord'; surely something he would not have done until there had been a change of heart. Second, Ananias called Saul 'brother'. This, of course, could have been used in the sense of a brother Israelite, although it is very doubtful if Ananias would have called Saul this, knowing all that he had done in the past. Added to this evidence, the original account in Acts 9 shows that Paul was healed and filled with the Holy Spirit *before* he was baptised. The latter is a clear sign of God's saving work within Paul and so his baptism would have been an outward testimony to what had happened within.

There are some other scriptures we need to note:

1 Corinthians 1:17

> "For Christ did not send me to baptize, but to
> preach the gospel, not in cleverness of
> speech, that the cross of Christ should not be
> made void."

Paul explains here that he was sent by the Lord to preach the gospel, to bring the message of true salvation to the Gentiles. However, he also clearly says that he was not sent to baptise! I believe that this verse shows beyond any doubt that baptism is not essential for salvation. The way Paul speaks about the two acts shows that baptism is not included in the good news of the gospel. This, as we have already seen, fits in with his definition of the main declaration of the gospel in 1 Corinthians 15.

Acts 16:31

> "And they said, 'Believe in the Lord Jesus, and you shall be saved, you and your household.'"

Paul, in response to the jailer's impassioned plea, tells him how he can be saved: "Believe on the Lord Jesus, and you shall be saved." After complying with this command, the jailer had an obvious change in his attitude to the prisoners. Those that he should be guarding with his life, he takes and washes and bandages their wounds; only then were he and his family baptised. As we have seen, the basic presentation of the gospel always includes repentance and believing, and baptism is only mentioned sometimes. As such it becomes clear what the Lord is saying is essential for salvation.

John 3:5

> "Jesus answered, 'Truly, truly, I say to you, unless one is born of water and the Spirit, he cannot enter into the kingdom of God.'"

Some groups would seek to use the phrase, 'born of water', to show that to be born again we must be baptised. However, it is important to note that Jesus did not say, 'unless a man is born of baptism'. Jesus often spoke figuratively about water (see John 4:14 and 7:38), and there is no reason to believe that he was talking about baptism in John 3. Titus 3:5 also uses the phrase 'the washing of regeneration', but again there is nothing to link this to a specific act of baptism. The context of the verse would seem to rule out any act that we can do. Salvation is not based on our deeds but on God's mercy.

Always Being Ready!

We can sum this section up with another quotation from Bancroft's book:

> "The Scriptures represent baptism to be, not the means, but only the sign of regeneration. For this reason only believers – that is, perhaps giving credible evidence of being regenerated – were baptized (Acts 8:12). Not external baptism, but the conscientious turning of the soul to God, which baptism symbolizes, saves us (1 Peter 3:21). Some New Testament verses such as Acts 2:38 and Col 2:12 are to be explained upon the principle that regeneration, the inward change, and baptism, the outward sign of that change, were regarded as only different sides or aspects of the same fact and either side or aspect might, therefore be described in terms derived from the other." – E. H. Bancroft. *Christian Theology.* p. 248.

Section 4

Overview of what some Cults Believe

11- Jehovah's Witnesses

Where did they come from?

The forming of the modern-day Watchtower Bible and Tract Society of the Jehovah's Witnesses began with Charles Taze Russell in the 1870s. At this time, after a chequered religious youth, he began studying the Bible. Under the influence of the Second Adventists, he soon was proclaiming 1874 as the date of the return of Jesus Christ.

1874 did not see the Lord appearing on earth, but, not to be outdone, Russell found a new and interesting teaching. He discovered the Greek word *parousia*, meaning the presence of Christ, and changed his story to say that Christ did come, but invisibly. However, there was still not long to wait, because the kingdom of God would now be set up on earth in 1914.

Six thousand copies of the first edition of *Zion's Watch Tower*, the forerunner of today's Watchtower, were printed in July 1879. At first it was monthly and sometimes bimonthly, but by the early 1900s it was being printed twice a month as it still is today. The Watchtower Bible and Tract Society was formed in 1881 and incorporated in 1884.

Russell died in October 1916 having already changed the date for the start of the kingdom's earthly reign from 1914 to 1915. This was an action that the second president, Joseph Franklin Rutherford, was going to follow on several occasions. He also caused quite a stir by changing many doctrines that Russell had held dear, resulting in hundreds or maybe even thousands leaving the Society. It is an interesting fact that many major doctrines of the Watchtower Society today stem from the second president, Rutherford, and not from its founder, Russell.

Always Being Ready!

As a result of certain passages in his book, *The Finished Mystery*, Rutherford served a short sentence for espionage in Atlanta Penitentiary. However, his release from prison only served as an opportunity to give a new impetus to the Society. Today, Jehovah's Witnesses are taught that this release from prison on earth in 1918 heralded the first resurrection of the 144,000 to heaven in the same year.

1919 is seen as the year that Jehovah looked down on earth and chose His one organisation, the Watchtower Bible and Tract Society. Of course there is no proof for this event one way or the other, but there seems to be much circumstantial evidence that it did not happen. Not least that some of the major doctrinal issues that the Society teach now, for instance, Jesus died on a stake, Christmas is pagan and Christ returned invisibly in 1914; they did not believe in 1919. If they were Jehovah's chosen organisation because of what they believed in 1919 then they are not that organisation today and if they are His organisation today then Jehovah made a mistake in 1919!

In 1920 the book *Millions Now Living Will Never Die* was published. This predicted the return to earth of the Old Testament princes, to rule over God's kingdom, in 1925. Men such as Abraham, Isaac and Jacob would return to life and be the leaders of the Great Crowd on earth. So sure were they of their return that by 1930 they even had a house prepared for them in San Diego, California.

1941 saw the release of the book *Children*. At the annual convention that year young people were presented with a copy of the book. In a keynote speech they were then instructed to use it on the door-to-door ministry, in the remaining *months* before Armageddon. The book counselled that whatever happened they should make sure that they did not get married before that battle started.

Since Rutherford's death in 1942, three further presidents have come and gone and these days the President is only a figurehead. A group of 'other sheep' not the 'anointed' are now taking the brunt of the day-to-day running of the Society, including receiving the various court summonses over blood and child abuse. It appears, of course, that this was the reason for changing the Governing Body to be the spiritual leaders but the official version would say otherwise.

Nathan Homer Knorr followed Rutherford and he was largely responsible for making the 'organisational structure' that the Society has today. He was followed by Frederick W. Franz, who died in December 1992.

In Franz's years as president, the Society went through several traumas. First, came the expectation built up over 1975 as another date for the kingdom of God to be set up on earth. Approximately a quarter of a million Witnesses left the Society when this date proved another disappointment.

Second, the organisation was rocked in the early 1980s when many from the American 'Bethel' headquarters left the Society or were disfellowshipped, the term the Society use for expulsion. This group included Ray Franz, the President's nephew and one-time member of the governing body. The trouble started when different groups began reading the Bible without the help of Watchtower publications. They started questioning the authority and the teachings of the Society, and many found a true relationship with Jesus Christ.

As indicated already, the Society is facing many traumas over the areas of blood transfusions and paedophiles, with legal action being taken against the Society. Latest news and information can be found on the Reachout website - http://www.reachouttrust.org

All these facts, however, may not cause the average Witness immediately to doubt and leave the Society. First, they will usually not listen readily to anyone outside the organisation, and second, they will believe all the explanations given by the Governing Body. Yet, knowing their history, we can lovingly sow doubts concerning the fact that they believe this has been constituted as 'God's sole visible channel on earth today'.

Always Being Ready!

Who are they?

Jehovah's Witnesses are often viewed with suspicion and mistrust, but probably over 90% of those that you meet will be sincere and very zealous. They will believe that unless you become a Witness you will not be in Jehovah's new kingdom.

Most are in the Society for genuine and positive reasons. Often they joined at a time of crisis in their life. Many would have cried out, "Oh God, help me!" A few days later there would be a knock at the door and two very pleasant Witnesses would begin to bring God's answer. They would have found loving, caring people who would spend many hours explaining the Bible to them.

What they did not realise, though, as they started on their round of five hours of meetings, two to three hours on the doors, and several hours of preparation each week, was that they were losing their own identity. Many did not realise what the subtle process of questions and answers from the Society's own literature was doing to them. Through the teaching that the only people who really hear God are the Governing Body and that independent thinking is of the devil, individuals stop thinking for themselves and become 'organisational robots'.

Average Witnesses do not think for themselves in any area of life – they simply check what the Governing Body has written in the latest *Watchtower*, or *Awake!* magazines, or in the latest book released. In this way they have no personal relationship with Jesus, only with the 'organisation'. However, as they equate serving the 'organisation' with serving Jehovah, this does not present a problem to them.

Their commitment to Jehovah's Organisation/Jehovah is total and puts some Christians to shame. They do not see refusing blood transfusions as wasting a life, but rather as laying down their life for Jehovah's sake.

What do they believe?

There is only one *God*, the Father and Creator. His name is Jehovah and all true Christians should use this, His personal name. He alone is to be worshipped. In the early church He had one *organisation* with its Governing Body in Jerusalem. Today He will only have one organisation, the Watchtower Bible & Tract Society with its governing body.

Jesus is unique in that he is the first created being of Jehovah. He is not eternal and as such he cannot be God although he is a lesser god. As their translation of John 1:1 shows, he is 'a god', whereas Jehovah is *the* God. They also believe that Jesus is only ever called 'mighty' but Jehovah is referred to as 'almighty'. Other verses, especially in the New Testament, for example Revelation 3:14, are mistranslated to show that Jesus is created. Still others are explained away by the various publications which a Witness must use to help them understand Scripture.

Jesus is also the same person as Michael the archangel. Wherever we read in Scripture that Michael did something, it is the same as reading that Jesus did it. After He created Jesus, Jehovah used him to create all other things.

The *Holy Spirit* is a force and extension of the power of Jehovah. He is not a person but an 'it' and is often likened to electricity. The conclusion is, therefore, that as He is not even a person, He certainly cannot be God. Gifts of the Holy Spirit are not for today and anyone manifesting them must have received the enabling from Satan and not God.

The *Trinity*, as can be clearly seen from the above beliefs, must be a pagan doctrine. It is not taught in the Bible and none of the early church fathers ever mentioned it. Any Christian who believes in the Trinity is actually part of the 'worldwide empire of Babylon', Satan's kingdom. This is one reason Jehovah's Witnesses believe that everything that goes on inside a church is of the devil.

Jehovah's Witnesses will believe that their doctrine is the true teaching of the *Bible*. However, their translation, the *New World Translation*, although being 80-90% the Word of God, has twisted many key verses. Just about every verse that shows the deity of Christ has been altered and they have regularly translated 'in Christ' as 'in *union with* Christ'.

Always Being Ready!

There is no justification for this in the Greek, as their own *Kingdom Interlinear Translation* shows, but it does remove the Witness from the necessity of a personal and intimate relationship with Christ.

Although lip-service will be paid to *salvation by grace*, the reality is that the organisation provides salvation in the end. Only active Jehovah's Witnesses in the organisation will survive the battle of Armageddon, the outpouring of God's wrath on the earth. All the rest of the people will be annihilated. *Hell* does not exist and all who are annihilated obviously have no hope of a resurrection.

Theirs is a two-tier salvation. Only the *144,000*, an élite chosen group, will be with Jesus in heaven and the rest, the *'great crowd'* or 'other sheep' will have eternal life on a paradise earth.

After Armageddon, all who are counted worthy will be *resurrected* (see next paragraph) and given a second chance of salvation on paradise earth. They must be loyal to the directives of the 144,000 and Jesus ruling in heaven. After being obedient for 1,000 years they must then make sure they are not in the group that the Bible says will follow Satan. Even with a second chance, the outcome is hardly certain.

Man does not have an *eternal spirit*; at death he ceases to exist and simply becomes a memory to God. If he is a 'worthy one', God will in time remember and resurrect him to have a second chance in the millennium. This act is more akin to recreating as there is nothing actually left to resurrect.

Dates and *chronology* have always been important to the Watchtower Society. Many dates have been suggested for the setting up of God's kingdom on earth, but all have proved false. 1914 has always been one of their key dates but it has had different meanings over the years. Originally it was the setting up of the kingdom of God on earth 40 years after Jesus returned invisibly in 1874. Today it is the actual date for the invisible return of Jesus Christ to take his throne in the heavens. It is also now the end of the Gentile Times and the beginning of the time of the end. It was also, until a few years ago, the year of the generation that would not totally pass away until Armageddon came. However due to the time scale, this has now been altered.

Other beliefs that should be mentioned include the fact that they do not celebrate Christmas, Easter or birthdays. Jesus did not die on the cross but a stake. God forbids blood transfusions.

A guide to helpful material that will provide more detailed information can be found on p.209.

Sharing the gospel

I hope by now we have seen that the Witness on the doorstep is a divine appointment rather than a perishing nuisance. The least we can do is bring the conversation around to our testimony of Jesus. However, please do not talk about your salvation so that the Witness can dismiss it as an emotional experience. Wherever possible, relate your experience to the commands and promises found in God's Word.

We will give just a couple of examples of how conversations could go. The wording may not be exactly what is said, but you should get the drift and be ready to come in at the right time.

WITNESS: Are you aware what a terrible state the world is in? It is just as the Lord said in Matthew 24 ...

CHRISTIAN: Yes, I know Satan is causing many problems for humanity today, but Jesus has told us that we do not need to be overcome by fear. He has said that He gives us peace and victory. Please let me explain what happened in my life...

WITNESS: It is interesting that you said you attend the local church. It is good to find those interested in spiritual things today. However, we do have to be careful that we are receiving the right teaching. For instance, so many churches today teach the doctrine of the Trinity but did you know that this booklet clearly shows that it is a pagan doctrine? It is illogical, isn't it, how can Jesus be the same as Jehovah?

CHRISTIAN: I do believe the Bible teaches the doctrine of the Trinity, although I do not think that this is the main problem. Did you know that the Bible tells us that God accepts us on what we think of Jesus? Do you agree?

WITNESS: Our view of Jesus is important but not as important as what we think of Jehovah.

CHRISTIAN: Okay. But we show what we think of Jehovah the Father by obeying His instructions. Note what Jehovah says we should think of Jesus (point out relevant scriptures, for example, Matthew 17:5). I would also like to tell you what happened when I came to know Jesus as Jehovah wants us to

(Young Christians may not be able to do anything more at this stage. However, for more mature Christians, to go on to give a simple presentation like the following will be very helpful for the Witness.)

Could we look at John 20:28 please? This is the second time that Jesus has appeared to the disciples but the first time that Thomas sees Him. In verse 27 Jesus is encouraging him to believe and Thomas' immediate response is to acknowledge Jesus as "My Lord and my God." (This seems fairly clear until we realise what the Witness had been taught. The Society say that either Thomas got so excited he blasphemed or he said, "My Lord", looking at Jesus, and "My God", looking up to Jehovah in heaven.)

Could we look at the verse carefully please? First, it clearly says Thomas said to him (Jesus) both statements. Second, the Watchtower *Greek Interlinear Version* (KIT) shows the words Thomas used. He said *ho theos* and the literal English rendering underneath is 'the God of me'.

This is the Greek phrase that the Watchtower Society say is used exclusively of Jehovah God. Jesus is called not just 'a god' but 'the God'. If this were not true, He would have had to rebuke Thomas in John 20:29. Instead He commends all those who will believe the same as Thomas believed. Notice, please, that this verse 28 is sandwiched between 27 and 29, both of which encourage belief. What would all the apostles have believed from these words?

You will probably not be able to rattle this off without interruption, but don't worry, and when you have completed this presentation, note that we have established that the Jesus of the Bible is different from the Jesus of the Watchtower. Now we must also establish that we need a different relationship with Jesus. To do this we turn to John 3:3.

Immediately the Witness will dismiss this verse as just for the 144,000 heavenly ones, but let's look again carefully at the verse.

First, get the Witness to read the end of the verse in the Watchtower Bible (NWT) – 'see the kingdom of God'. Most Witnesses will actually translate it in their minds as, 'enter the kingdom of heaven' because it is the 144,000. Make the point though that the verse says 'see the kingdom of God' and ask, "Don't you expect to see the kingdom of God?"

Every Witness has the hope that they will see the kingdom on earth. This, then, is for you, isn't it? But what has to happen to see the kingdom – we must be born again!

The Witness will not like thinking about being born again because it's only for the 144,000 and if anyone else claims it then it must be some 'voodoo' act. Use illustrations such as the caterpillar that longed to fly and spent all its time running up long cabbage leaves and jumping off, only to fall to the ground. However, one day things started to get dark and hard and it seemed to have died but suddenly there was light at the end of the tunnel and finally emerging – it could fly. It could now live in a dimension that it could never live in before; it had been 'born again' as a butterfly.

Always Being Ready!

Remind them that they do know of people (the remnant of the 144,000 on earth) who are to be born again. Show that to be born again is an act that enables them to live in a new dimension in God's heavenly kingdom. It's no 'voodoo' experience but a work of God in our lives, which is necessary if we are to see God's kingdom.

Finally point out that their Bible says 'unless anyone'. Are you an *anyone*? If this is only for the 144,000, then God is a liar when He says 'anyone'. What is the only way you will ever see the kingdom of God – earthly or heavenly?

There are many other ways that we can bring Jesus to the Jehovah's Witness and details of other helps will be found in the 'Conclusion' chapter. The important thing is that we spend some time preparing our notes now, so that we are ready when the knock, knock arrives.

12 - Latter-day Saints

Where did they come from?

The Church of Jesus Christ of the Latter-day Saints, or Mormons as they are more often known, had their beginnings in the north of New York State in the early 1800s. A fourteen-year-old boy by the name of Joseph Smith received a vision of Jesus and His Father.

The story goes that there was revival in the churches all around and Joseph wanted to know which church to join. Determined to find the answer, he went into the forest to ask God to tell him which church was right. He received the unexpected response that all churches were apostate and that he was not to join any of them but rather he should start his own. Thus began The Church of Jesus Christ of Latter-day Saints, contrasting with the Former-day saints that Mormons believe went into complete apostasy. The church that began with the pouring out of the Holy Spirit at Pentecost failed. Joseph Smith became the founding prophet of the only true church on earth today.

The official version of the beginnings of Mormonism is found in *The Pearl of Great Price*. However, problems arise because of several other Mormon-verified versions of the first vision. Discrepancies between these versions include: what age was Joseph when he received the vision? Whom did he see? The Lord of glory, two unidentified persons, angels, or the Father and the Son? How many persons were there: one or two? Was there a revival in progress in the area, or not? All these problems have led to questioning the very foundations of Mormonism.

All this cannot be dismissed as insignificant because the first vision is very important to Mormons. The following quotations from their own books show this.

> "The church stands or falls on the reality of this first vision." – Joseph Fielding Smith, *Doctrines of Salvation*, Vol. 1. p. 188.

Always Being Ready!

> "This vision was the most important event that had taken place in all world history since the day of Christ's ministry." – Bruce McConkie, *Mormon Doctrine*, p. 284.

The golden plates

This first vision is said to have taken place in 1820, but it was not until 1823 that the next stage took place. In that year Joseph had a further heavenly visitation, telling him about the existence of the golden plates that contained what we know today as the *Book of Mormon*. On the following day he located the plates but was not allowed to take them home until September 1827, when the real work began. Although it took about a year to translate the *Book of Mormon*, most of the work was completed in the last three months when Oliver Cowdrey was helping Joseph. Until then Joseph had two other helpers in the translation work, Emma, his wife, and Martin Harris. We use the word "translate" but it could not be achieved without the help of some supernatural means; the plates were written in 'Reformed Egyptian,' a language that does not exist!

Translating 'God's book' was not without its problems. *Doctrine and Covenants* 3:9,10 tells of God's displeasure with Joseph Smith because he lost 116 pages of the original translated manuscript of the *Book of Mormon*. Martin Harris lost the pages but he thought that Joseph could just retranslate them. The truth was undoubtedly that Joseph could not be sure that it would be the same text if the missing pages were ever found. However, God answered the problem by leading him to another section of the plates that dealt with the same period but in a more spiritual way!

The contents of the Book of Mormon

The *Book of Mormon* is the story of a Hebrew prophet, Lehi, whom the Lord ordered to flee from Jerusalem. He left with his family around 600 BC and they found their way to a new

156

land that is today known as America. Later the descendants of two of Lehi's sons, the Nephites and the Lamanites, fought each other. The Lamanites had departed from the Lord, but the Nephites remained faithful and had kept a detailed history of their dealings. Mormon, one of the last remaining Nephites, wrote an account of their history on the golden plates and gave them into the hands of his son Moroni. Moroni buried them in the Hill Cumorah, near Palmyra, New York, around AD 438, to prevent them from falling into the hands of the Lamanites. He was hiding from the Lamanites at the time and expected to be killed soon after he had buried the plates.

The very foundation of the story of the *Book of Mormon* is today being brought into question by scientific DNA evidence (see a "Guide to Helpful Materials" on p.209 for more details). Native Americans do not descend from peoples from the Middle East, but from an area surrounding Lake Baikal in Siberia before their migration to the New World over 14,000 years ago. (See Simon G Southerton's *Losing a Lost Tribe, Native Americans, DNA, and the Mormon Church*, pub. Signature Books, Sept. 2004 - reviewed at http://www.signaturebooks.com/Losing.htm).

The producing of the Book of Mormon

Mormons will claim that producing the *Book of Mormon* in such a short time, proves that it is from God and not from man. However, there are many other theories that do not include God's help. One suggestion is that the manuscript of a book stolen from the printers became the basis of the story. Another is that, as his mother related, Joseph used to spin great yarns that kept the family enthralled, and so it was a natural talent. Both could be part of the explanation. What is certain is that the *Book of Mormon* contains some 27,000 words from the King James Version of the Bible. This shows that using other manuscripts would not be out of the question.

Always Being Ready!

We should probably not rule out some supernatural help either, but from which source? Smith himself admitted using a peep-stone (a type of crystal-ball) to try to find buried treasure. David Whitmer, who was closely involved with the work of producing the *Book of Mormon*, and Joseph's wife Emma both confirmed that Joseph used a peep-stone in a hat to accomplish the translation (other stories talk of 'magical spectacles'). The supernatural help through the peep-stone would not come from God.

The authenticating of the *Book of Mormon*

As the *Book of Mormon* contains such detailed history, it should not be difficult to prove the truth of the book through archaeology, geography, etc. Unfortunately, for modern-day Mormons, there is little, if any, evidence in these fields that can be used to support the *Book of Mormon*.

For instance, Alma 11:4-19 mentions eight different coins, but not a single example of even one of them has ever been discovered. Ether 9:18-19 mentions several animals, traces of which have never been found in that place at that time. Indeed, two animals mentioned, the cureloms and cumoms have never been discovered anywhere, or at any time.

From New York to Salt Lake City

While the translating work was continuing, the headquarters of the Mormons were first briefly in New York and then in Pennsylvania before they moved to Kirtland, Ohio in 1831. The State of Missouri became known as the land of Zion, and the first Mormon temple site was dedicated there in August 1831 and finally opened in 1836.

Continual persecution forced the church to leave Missouri and they settled in Commerce, Illinois, in 1839. The town of Commerce was renamed Nauvoo and the Mormons experienced rapid growth but not without problems. In 1844, several discontented members printed charges of polygamy and strange doctrines against Joseph Smith and the Mormon Church, in the *Nauvoo Expositor*. Enraged, Joseph Smith incited a mob to destroy the printing press and this led to his arrest and imprisonment in the Carthage town jail. Joseph Smith died from a gunshot wound when a mob came to the jail to lynch him on 27 June 1844.

Under Brigham Young, the Mormons continued west until they reached what today is known as Utah. Here they settled and built Salt Lake City that is still their very impressive headquarters today.

In 1837, the first Mormon converts were recorded in Britain. They were baptised in the River Ribble in Preston. In the early days many families left through the ports of Liverpool and Bristol to go to the USA. Today, the Mormons claim to be one of the fastest growing groups in Britain and currently have approximately 180,000 members.

There are two temples in Britain, one on the borders of Surrey and Sussex at Lingfield, and the other in Chorley, Lancs. The temple is where their secret ceremonies take place and is different from the regular meeting places you see in many towns.

Who are they?

Mormons will, for the most part, be genuine and believe what they say, but they will be deceived themselves. Many you meet will be Americans, undertaking their missionary service.

At some point they will probably have been given a *Book of Mormon* and asked to read certain verses. They will then have been told to pray and ask God to confirm that this is the word of God. Many at that point will feel the 'burning in the bosom' and receive the testimony that Mormonism is true, and Joseph Smith is the prophet. This 'spiritual' experience will often take precedence over any number of facts revealed to them.

Comparatively few Mormons will have gone through special temple ceremonies and received 'holy underwear' containing Masonic symbols, although all the missionaries do so. Maybe they will have been sealed in marriage for eternity or have been baptised for dead relatives. To them Mormonism is the only true religion and the only way to God.

Official figures for the United Kingdom indicate that there are 176,998 Church members, 45 Stakes, 274 Wards, 99 Branches, 7 Missions and 2 Temples.

What do they believe?

Before we can look at what they believe we need to understand how they arrive at these beliefs. We will therefore deal with the section on the *Bible* first.

Mormons have three books that they call Scriptures: the *Book of Mormon, Doctrine and Covenants* and the *Pearl of Great Price*. They will also quote the Bible and will produce reference editions that are cross-linked to the Bible. However, where the Bible and the Book of Mormon disagree, their eighth *Article of Faith* makes it clear which they will choose:

> "We believe the Bible to be the word of God as far **as it is translated correctly;** we also believe the *Book of Mormon* to be the word of God." (Emphasis added.)

Many Mormons will say that they accept the King James Version of the Bible. However, the front cover of the handout edition of the *Book of Mormon* has in big gold letters, 'Another Testament of Jesus Christ'. Why do we need another? What has this Testament added that was not in the original?

Twice in *Doctrine and Covenants* (20:8,9 & 27:5) we read that the "fullness of the gospel" is found within the *Book of Mormon*. This means that the *Doctrine and Covenants* and the *Pearl of Great Price* can only expand on the *Book of Mormon* but cannot add anything. However, as we will show most of their major doctrines are not found within the *Book of*

Mormon and some are even contradicted by it. Mormons will explain this by progressive revelation through the Living Prophet of the church. The Living Prophet can speak fresh 'scripture', thus adding to or, indeed, taking away from the revelation up to that point. Many changes have been made to Mormonism since the *Book of Mormon* first appeared. Even the *Book of Mormon* has undergone nearly 4,000 changes since the first 'inspired' edition in 1830.

The Mormon will try to 'prove' that the *Book of Mormon* should be held up alongside the Bible by showing that the Bible foretold the *Book of Mormon*. Ezekiel 37:15-20, they say, shows that the *Book of Mormon* is one of the joined rods, the other rod being the Bible. However, this is an interpretation because the Bible clearly shows that they are rods - not books - and that they represent two parts of Israel coming together, not two books that have different stories. With such a foundation for their belief in what is scripture, it will not be a surprise to find the confusion in their teachings today.

God was once a man. This is one of their teachings not found in the *Book of Mormon* but it is found in Joseph Fielding Smith's, The *Teaching of the Prophet Joseph Smith*, pp. 344/5. This belief alone shows that the Mormon idea of God is unscriptural but, because of the Christian words and ideas they use, it may at first appear Christian. One God, who was once a man and not a trinity, is not only denied by the Bible but also by the *Book of Mormon.*

> "For I know that God is not a partial God, neither a changeable being; but he is unchangeable from all eternity to eternity." – Moroni 8:18.

> "And now, behold, this is the doctrine of Christ, and the only and true doctrine of the Father, and of the Son, and of the Holy Ghost, which is one God, without end. Amen." – 2 Nephi 31:21.

Always Being Ready!

> "... the Father, and the Son, and the Holy
> Ghost are one; and I am in the Father, and
> the Father in me. and the Father and I are
> one. And thus will the Father hear record
> of me, and the Holy Ghost will bear record
> unto him of the Father and me; for the
> Father, and I, and the Holy Ghost are one."
> – 3 Nephi 11:27.36.

Despite this clear teaching from the *Book of Mormon*, they do not just deny the *Trinity*; they add that **all men can become gods**. Again this is found in *The Teachings of the Prophet Joseph Smith*, pp. 346/7 but denied by the *Book of Mormon*.

God lives near the planet Kolob according to Bruce McConkie in *Mormon Doctrine*, p. 428. In the same way every Mormon man exalted to godhood will receive his own planet to rule over.

Jesus in the spirit realm was the brother of Lucifer. He became an ordinary man, was married while he lived on earth, and had several children.

> "Now, remember from this time forth, and
> for ever, that Jesus Christ was not
> begotten by the Holy Ghost." – Brigham
> Young, *Journal of Discourses*, Vol. 1, p.
> 51.

Jesus is talked about especially in Christian countries, but the key to Mormonism is not Jesus Christ. The central figure is Joseph Smith as the following quotation from *The Missionaries' Preparation Guide to Home Studies* shows.

> "The main focus of this discussion should be
> the *Book of Mormon* and the Prophet
> Joseph Smith. ... After the discussion, the
> investigators strongest impression should be
> of the *Book of Mormon* and the Prophet
> Joseph Smith."

The *Holy Spirit* is a person and part of the Mormon Godhead. There is controversy, however, because he is both "a personage of spirit" *and* a god. However, in order to become a god, he would have had to pass through mortality.

There are also writings within Mormonism that show that the death of Jesus Christ is not sufficient for salvation.

> "It is true that the blood of the Son of God was shed for sins through the fall and those committed by men, yet men can commit sins which it can never remit." - Brigham Young, *Journal of Discourses*. Vol.4. p. 53.

The Mormon scriptures also show very clearly (emphasis added) that their *salvation is by works* and not by faith alone.

> "...it is by grace that we are saved, *after all we can do*." – 2 Nephi 25:23.

> "We believe that through the Atonement of Christ, all mankind may be *saved, by obedience* to the laws and ordinances of the Gospel." – *Third Article of Faith*.

Not a Mormon alive knows every law and ordinance, but some that they will seek to obey are:

The *Word of Wisdom*. This is found in *Doctrine & Covenants* 89 and it actually forbids strong drinks, hot drinks, and tobacco. In modern-day belief this has been changed to forbidding the drinking of tea, coffee and caffeine drinks. Mormons must abide by the *Word of Wisdom* to prove themselves worthy of great joy in the next life. (See Study Guide 4 *Eternal Progression*).

Secret temple ceremonies. Not every Mormon is allowed to go to the temple, only those who are found worthy and have received their 'Temple Recommend'. This is a signed pass, valid for one year, which allows the holder into any temple in the world.

Always Being Ready!

Baptism for the dead. This instruction is found in *Doctrine & Covenants* 128:17,18. First, you must undertake genealogy work to discover the names of your dead relatives. This has led some Mormons into occultic experiences because they are concentrating on the dead. Mormons still claim, especially to Christians, that 1 Corinthians 15:29 is their authority for baptising the dead. Investigation shows that the *Book of Mormon* disagrees with this belief. Alma 34:34,35 tells us that everything is decided before death and so baptism for the dead is futile. Added to this 2 Nephi 28:22,23 shows that there is no opportunity to be saved after death because then comes the judgement.

Tithing. This teaching found in *Doctrine & Covenants* 119:4 is vital if a Mormon wants to go through the temple and receive his exaltation to godhood. Accurate records are kept of every penny given. With special tithing, funds, etc., Mormons can give up to 30% of their income to the church.

In the Mormon ***afterlife*** there are three heavens or kingdoms described in *Doctrine & Covenants* 131. The Celestial kingdom is reserved exclusively for those who believe and are obedient to the Mormon gospel. Only those in this kingdom have any hope of becoming gods and ruling over their own planet. Many Mormon men are striving to be in such a position.

The Terrestrial kingdom is the second level and it is reserved for good men and women of all religions, who have not embraced Mormonism. All the wicked and degraded will inhabit the lowest level called the Telestial kingdom. Clearly there are two salvations: a general one for all 'good' people, and a specific one for the 'élite' of Mormonism.

Currently ***polygamy*** is not an official practice of the Latter-day Saints, but remains a doctrine and many believe it will be practised again in the future. They only gave it up 'officially' because of the law of the land and their eternal future still involves being a god of a planet with many goddess wives. What needs to be underlined, though, is that according to the *Book of Mormon* polygamy should never have been accepted in the first place:

> "Behold David and Solomon truly had
> many wives and concubines, which thing
> was abominable before me, saith the
> Lord." – Jacob 2:24.

Mormons do not look upon themselves as just another denomination, but uniquely and completely *the Church* of Jesus Christ.

> "All other churches are entirely destitute of
> all authority from God. ... And any person
> who shall ... receive a holy ordinance of
> the gospel from the ministers of any of
> these apostate churches will be sent down
> to hell with them." – Apostle Orson Pratt,
> *The Seer*, p.255.

Non-Mormons will be forever barred from the close presence of God. They lack the required certificate with the authorising signature!

> "From the day the Priesthood was taken
> from the earth to the windup scene of all
> things, every man and woman must have
> the certificate of Joseph Smith as a
> passport to their entrance into the mansion
> where God and Christ are." – Brigham
> Young, *Journal of Discourses*, Vol. 7, p.
> 289.

Eventually this must result in a direct challenge to Jesus Christ because He is not enough. Without Joseph Smith, the church he founded, the *Book of Mormon*, the temple ritual, the observance of all Mormon Church regulations, including the daily wearing of the sacred underwear, the close presence of God will be denied us. It is not enough to believe in the Lord Jesus Christ, receive Him as personal Saviour, and seek to live according to the teachings of the Bible.

Always Being Ready!

> "Full salvation is attained by virtue of knowledge. ... Without continuous revelation ... there would be no salvation. If it had not been for Joseph Smith and the restoration, there would be no salvation. There is no salvation outside The Church of Jesus Christ of Latter-day Saints." – *Doctrines of Salvation*, Vol. 2, quoted by Bruce McConkie, *Mormon Doctrine*, 1988, p. 670.

It is important to know that many of these doctrines will not be revealed when the Mormon first calls at the door but all the above points are clearly documented in Mormon literature.

Communication

Some Mormons still call from door-to-door and therefore you may find them on your doorstep, but there will be many parts of the country where this will not happen. Specific contacts are sought these days and most do not just call 'cold'. Advertising in *Readers' Digest*, TV magazines, etc., produces the required names and addresses. The advertisements sometimes offer the *Book of Mormon* as a companion version to the Bible. Alternatively, they offer a message on cassette tape, but both will have an invitation to write for a free copy. Whatever is offered, it will usually not be sent by post, but will be delivered personally.

In recent years Mormons have also made two videos on aspects of the life of Christ and these are advertised on certain television channels. The videos appear to be true to Scripture and often are, but this is its deceptive nature. Local Mormons have a list of all who write for these videos and will either deliver them or call on a follow-up visit.

Another place you might meet the Mormons is in your local shopping centre, conducting a questionnaire. The questions asked will vary, depending on the time of year or national events taking place. Finally, you will be asked a question that suggests that, if there is something better, surely you would want to hear about it. An appointment would then be made to visit you.

Once in your home the missionaries will want to take you through an introductory course of six lessons. These will reveal what they want you to know, at that point, about Mormonism.

Sharing the gospel

As Mormons are clearly working for their salvation, do find ways of emphasising the grace of God. Remember, though, when talking with them, that they have been taught that Joseph Smith and the *Book of Mormon* are to be the central themes of their discussions. Jesus Christ, however, is still the only way to God and we need to find ways to talk about Him. There are many relevant ways to do this and here is one suggestion using the *Book of Mormon*. Set the scene by showing that the *Book of Mormon* teaches that the Bible is true and contains the Gospel:

> "I beheld other books, which came forth by the power of the Lamb from the Gentiles unto them, unto the convincing of the Gentiles and the remnant of the seed of my brethren, and also the Jews scattered upon the face of the earth, that the records of the prophets and of the twelve apostles of the Lamb are true. And the angel spake unto me, saying: These last records, which thou hast seen among the Gentiles, shall establish the truth of the first ..." – 1 Nephi 13:39-40.

You could also add that it teaches that new birth is essential:

> "And now behold, I ask you, my brethren of the church, have ye spiritually been born of

> God? Have you received his image in your countenances? Have ye experienced this mighty change in your hearts?" – Alma 5:14.

> "For, said he, I have repented of my sins, and have been redeemed of the Lord; behold I am born of the Spirit ... I am born of God." – Mosiah 27:24, 28.

This surely contradicts their *Third Article of Faith*, which as we have already shown, teaches that the Mormon gospel is one of keeping commandments and ordinances. This is also contrary to the gospel that Paul preached which is endorsed by the *Book of Mormon*, which is very strange because we read in *Doctrine & Covenants* 18:9 that early Mormons were, 'called even with that same calling with which he (Paul) was called'. Obviously they also must have believed what Paul believed. Paul tells us that he believes (1 Corinthians 15:1-4) that the gospel is all about Jesus. I Corinthians 1:14-17 also shows clearly that baptism was not in the true gospel Paul preached, and Galatians 1:6-10 shows what he said about any other gospel.

Highlight these differences, especially in the area of grace and works. Present what you know about the grace of Jesus (2 Corinthians 8:9) and that we cannot do even one thing to receive salvation (Ephesians 2:8-9)

In the light of these differences and because only one can be preaching the truth, ask if together you could answer the following questions from the *Book of Mormon* and the Bible.

Are we justified by the law?

2 Nephi 2:5, "... and by the law no flesh is justified", agrees with Romans 3:20, "because by the works of the Law no flesh will be justified ..." The answer is an emphatic No, we are not. Be ready to show (Galatians 3:24) that the purpose of the law is to act as our schoolteacher to lead us to Christ. Ask

the Mormon, have the commandments you have been taught led you to Christ?

Do we work for salvation or is it a free gift?

2 Nephi 2:4, "... and salvation is free", agrees with Ephesians 2:8-9, "For by grace you have been saved through faith; and that not of yourselves, it is the gift of God; not as a result of works that no one should boast." Salvation is a free gift.

In whom alone do we have Salvation?

2 Nephi 31:21, "... and there is none other way not name given under heaven whereby man can be saved..." agrees with Acts 4:12. "... There is no other name under heaven that has been given among men, by which we must be saved." There is agreement: the *only* name is Jesus.

Make each point slowly and carefully and ask whether the Bible and the *Book of Mormon* agree. Finally, offer a loving challenge to follow this clear testimony of the saving work of Christ alone. Bring this home further by sharing your testimony of new life in Christ.

There must be no adding to the simple and completed gospel of Jesus Christ. This is the solid ground we are encouraged to build on both in the Bible and the *Book of Mormon*.

Short presentation

Time is precious and, if you do not have much of it, on the next occasion you meet a Mormon, here is a short presentation that is often effective.

Turn to 1 Corinthians 15:29 and ask them if they believe that the true church of Christ today should be baptising for the dead. Let them explain their position and then tell them that you have a few problems over this and could they help you sort them out. Agree with them that the context of 1

Corinthians 15 is resurrection. Just as Paul has had to correct other problems in the Corinthian church, he now deals with the fact that some do not believe in the resurrection (15:12). In the correcting of this he mentions *those* who are baptising for the dead (15:29). However, in the next verse he talks about *we*, showing that Paul is not saying that the Christian church is baptising for the dead. Paul is emphasising that *those*, the pagans in Corinth, are doing it. His argument is that even the pagans believe there is a resurrection of the dead, so how much more should the Christians.

Having explained this, ask the Mormon, "Why does the Mormon church today, a group that claims to be the only true church, do what the pagans did in Corinth?"

By practising baptism for the dead, they have ignored both the teaching of the Bible and the *Book of Mormon* (see earlier, 'What they believe' section). Ask, 'What is your authority for baptising dead people into the Mormon Church?' The Bible clearly teaches that there is one life, one death and one judgement. After death it is too late to change one's mind.

A guide to helpful material that will provide more detailed information can be found on p.209.

13 – Christadelphians

Who are they?

As their name implies, the Christadelphians regard themselves as brethren of Christ, [Greek - *Christouadelphoi* - cf. Hebrews 2:11 & Colossians 1:2.]. They were founded in America through the teachings of an Englishman, Dr. John Thomas, who was born in London on 12 April 1805. In 1832 Thomas survived a shipwreck while on his way to New York and vowed that he would devote his life to searching Bible truths. Thomas was no stranger to Bible doctrine, being the son of a Congregationalist minister. However, he developed his own theories on the definition of many scriptures, with an emphasis on prophecy. His conclusions led him to disagree with mainstream Christianity on many central doctrines.

Development

When John Thomas first arrived in America, he joined himself to Alexander Campbell's Church of Christ but eventually left because he felt they were not preaching the whole truth. In 1844, he began a monthly magazine, *The Herald of the Future Age*.

Returning to England in 1848, Thomas published his ideas in *Elpis Israel* [The Hope of Israel] subtitled 'An Exposition of the Kingdom of God, with reference to the Time of the End and the Age to Come.' Thomas went back to America but made two further trips to England in 1862 and 1869. By then his book, *Elpis Israel* had helped to found several congregations that followed his teachings. Thomas died on 5 March 1871 and was buried in Brooklyn, New York. *Elpis Israel* is still highly appreciated by many Christadelphians and is sometimes presented to them at their baptism.

Birmingham, England, is not the headquarters of the movement, because there is not one, but it certainly is the area where much development took place. Each ecclesia or hall is independent, but the Birmingham Temperance Hall

Always Being Ready!

Fellowship was looked to for guidance at a very early age of the movement.

An early convert from Birmingham was Robert Roberts, baptised by Thomas in 1853, at the age of 14. Roberts a journalist, had a natural flair for communicating and wrote a series of pamphlets later published as, *Christendom Astray from the Bible*. After Thomas died, Roberts gradually became regarded as the leader. Roberts changed the title of a magazine he edited to *The Christadelphian*, and now with over 120 volumes it is regarded by many as the official mouthpiece of the organisation.

In Thomas' day, Christadelphians would not accept mainstream Christendom:

> "Convinced that this is the only scriptural constitution of the "one body" of which Jesus Christ is alone the head, and who has no personal representative on earth, we repudiate the popular churches and all their adjuncts, as no part thereof, and affirm that there is no salvation within the pale of any of them. ... We object to the fundamental doctrines of Christendom; the religion of the churches and chapels is a negation of Bible teaching on almost all points. ... We hold it to be the 'abominations of the earth' with all dissenting names and denominations, aggregately styled 'names of blasphemy', of which the European body politic, symbolised by the eight-headed, scarlet coloured beast is said to be full, (Rev.17:3)" – *We are the Christadelphians*, Thomas, pp.3, 6, 8.

Today, many Christadelphians would begrudgingly accept that those in other Christian groups could also be saved but, if you believe what Thomas said, there is no salvation in any other church.

Christadelphians

Christadelphians emphasise the disunities of Christendom but there are many splits within their movement. Their main forms of outreach are via telephone Bible Help Lines and a Bible Exhibition. The main topics for their outreaches are usually connected with Israel and the end times.

There are no 'official' statistics available for this group but one former Christadelphian estimates that there are approximately 30,000 members worldwide in the 'Central' fellowship with maybe up to another 5,000 in splinter groups. In Britain there are probably around 20,000 members, mainly found within the West Midlands area. Of this number it is estimated that 50% are traditional Christadelphians, 30% liberal and 20% are 'on-the-fence'.

Main Beliefs

Christadelphians are convinced by doctrine and many are firmly entrenched in their views. However, as some Christadelphians will have moved away from the original doctrines, it is always good practice to find out from them what they believe.

Christadelphians who continue in the original doctrines do not fully believe that Christ bore our sins at Calvary; *salvation* requires something from us:

> "The idea that Christ has borne our punishment and paid our debts, and that his righteousness is placed to our credit, and that all we have to do is believe it, is demoralising. It nullifies that other most important element of the truth ... that he only is righteous who doeth righteousness. It draws a veil over the truth that we have to 'work out our salvation' by a 'patient continuance in well-doing', and that he only that endureth to the end shall be saved. ... These blighting results are to be witnessed

> in all communities where the doctrine of a
> substitutionary sacrifice and an imputed
> righteousness holds sway." – *The Blood of
> Christ*, Roberts, undated reprint by the
> Christadelphians, p.30.

> "Christ has given Him [God the Father] no
> satisfaction, paid no debt in the
> commercial sense." – *The Slain Lamb*,
> Roberts, 1873, reprinted 1984, p.23.

Some would want to move away from this position today and
tone down what is said in the above quotes. Nevertheless,
they would still feel that we need to earn our salvation in
some way:

> " ... God offers the gift of eternal life ... But
> though we cannot earn it in the sense that
> we cannot pay the price commensurate to
> its value, God has set down conditions
> upon which alone His gift will be made.
> They constitute three steps to salvation:
> belief, baptism, obedience ... The reward
> for doing so is life eternal upon earth at
> Christ's coming." – *Baptism - Essential to
> Salvation*, Logos, p.15.

> "The only way to become a true Christian
> is to believe and be baptised into Christ. ...
> But before we can be baptised **we must
> understand** the teaching of the bible and
> believe it. ... **Many people need to study
> the Bible for at least a year or two
> before they understand** it well enough to
> be baptised... **Work hard** at your Bible
> study. It is worth making a big effort
> because **eternal life is a big prize**." –
> *Preparing for Baptism*, Christadelphian
> Bible Mission, undated, p.4. [Emphasis
> added.]

Christadelphians

Christadelphian salvation depends on an understanding of the Bible, baptism and the keeping of commandments. Clearly no Christadelphian can have assurance of salvation; at any time he can lose that hope of resurrection to eternal life on earth. One former Christadelphian put it as follows:

> "Christadelphians do not believe in salvation by works, yet they do not believe they are guaranteed salvation. Therefore, their salvation, they claim themselves, is conditional upon the keeping of the commandments of Christ. If they do not, they believe Christ will reject them when He separates the goats from the sheep. Of course, they pay lip-service to the fact that no-one can ultimately keep all the commandments. They also believe that Christ's sacrifice was not substitutionary and therefore only their sins before baptism are covered by Him and subsequent sins need to be repented of and forgiven for. Even then they are not often confident that they will be forgiven. In summary, there is much fear and doubt and a huge lack of understanding regarding God's Grace and Mercy. They do not believe their works save them, but they do believe baptism together with a strict following of the commandments of Christ (and all other New Testament laws) is how you can be saved, God willing." – Email to the author, June 1999.

This position is confirmed by their own publications, for instance:

> "When we believe the truth, we must next obey the commandments. If we fail to do this, the truth is not only no advantage to us, but will be to our condemnation. A

> community in which the commandments of Christ are not obeyed is not the house of Christ, but the synagogue of Satan, however correctly the truth may be discerned as a theory." – *Ecclesial Guide*, p.50

Whatever terminology is put on these words and however they are explained, we discover that unless we are baptised and unless we keep the commandments then we will not be saved but be rejected by Christ at the Judgement. Is this position Biblical?

We have already discussed the matter of baptism on page 135, but what about keeping the commandments? Galatians 5:1ff shows, among other Scriptures, a similar situation that Paul had to deal with. The Jewish believers were seeking to add to their salvation the necessity of keeping the commandment of circumcision. Paul shows just how futile this was.

Originally, the concept of *God* to a Christadelphian was summed up by Roberts as:

> "Philosophy or no philosophy, the Scriptures quoted plainly teach that the Father is a tangible person, in whom all the powers of the Universe converge." – *Christendom Astray*, Roberts, 1944, p.92.

This would not necessarily be a true reflection of what most believe today and maybe not even what Roberts believed in totality. Their 1975 booklet *Is There a God?* summed it up like this:

> "The nature of God is defined by the Lord Jesus Christ in the words: 'God is a Spirit. ...' He dwells personally in heaven. ... God has a located existence somewhere in the Universe. ... In the full sense, man is incapable of understanding what God is. ... Though personally located in heaven, God

is everywhere present by His spirit." –
Dawn Booklet No.1, 1975, pp.11, 12.

The Christadelphians strip **Jesus Christ** of His pre-existence, His deity, His title of Christ until His baptism, and the fullness of His atoning work on the cross.

"... the Bible clearly shows that Jesus had no existence prior to his birth in Bethlehem. ... Nowhere is it suggested that he existed before his birth. - Who is Jesus Christ?" – *Not a pre-existent Being, but Saviour of Mankind*, p.2.

"He was not God, neither a mere man, nor had he any existence prior to His supernatural birth." – *The Christadelphian*, vol., 1874, p.56.

"He was the Son of God, the manifestation of God by spirit-power, but not God himself." – *Christendom Astray*, Roberts, 1944, p.107.

"The Spirit descended upon him in bodily shape at his baptism... This was the anointing which constituted him Christ. ... before his anointing he was simply the 'body prepared' for the divine manifestation that was to take place through him." – *Christendom Astray*, Roberts, 1944, p.160.

There are a number of verses in the Bible that show that these definitions have problems. The first dealing with the pre-existence of Jesus is John 1:1.

"What John is stating, therefore, is that in the very beginning there existed the wisdom or purpose of God." – *The 'pre-existence' of Christ*, *Dawn* Booklet No.36, 1974, p.13.

Always Being Ready!

> "The Greek term translated 'word' [in John 1:1] is logos. It signifies the outward form of inward thought or reason, or the spoken word as illustrative of thought, wisdom and doctrine. The Bible teaching is that in the very beginning, God's purpose, wisdom or revelation was proclaimed through His Word. This Word was 'with God' in that it emanated from Him; it 'was God' in that it represented Him to mankind." – *Who is Jesus Christ?*, p.12

The web pages of Christian Apologetics and Research Ministry (CARM) at www.carm.org give this excellent answer to the Christadelphian claim:

> "The problem with their reasoning is not that their definition, in itself, is incorrect. For it can be said that the Word was indeed the wisdom and emanation from God. But that is not all it is saying. It is saying that the Word WAS God. Jesus IS the Word. He isn't simply a manifestation of some divine attribute or quality. Also, what about the context? In John 1:2-3 it says, "He was with God in the beginning. Through him all things were made; without him nothing was made that has been made" (NIV). First, the word is referred to as masculine. Wisdom in Proverbs 8:1-2 is personified as feminine. There is a difference. Second, the Word is who created all things (See also Col. 1:16-17). Of course, it is naturally understood that this does not include God Himself. But all that is made, has been made by the Word that became flesh. Third, the Word is referred to as a person, not a quality which the Christadelphians have imposed into the text."

In addition, other verses need to be explained. John 3:13 and 6:62 both show Jesus descending from heaven. How do the Christadelphians answer these? Again, p.11 of their booklet *The 'pre-existence' of Christ* explains:

> "... Christ came down from heaven in the sense that the Holy Spirit that begat him emanated from the Father in heaven, where Jesus has always existed in the mind and purpose of God."

But how can a thought in the mind of God be regarded as rich and consciously become poor as 2 Corinthians 8:9 so aptly describes the Lord Jesus' work? How can a thought in the mind of God consider whether equality with God is something to be grasped; or empty Himself; or take the form of a servant, being born in the likeness of men; all of which are clearly ascribed to Jesus in Philippians 2:5-7?

Jesus could boldly assert,

> "I came from the Father and have come into the world. I am leaving the world and going to the Father." – John 16:28.

Clearly the Scriptures show that Christ was pre-existent as a person and not just as a thought in the mind of His Father. There is however a further step we need to take. Was this person who was pre-existent, God?

If Jesus is not God, then we have a problem as to why many different people worshipped Him. Clearly Matthew 4:10 shows that only God is to receive worship but the two verses below are just examples of the many times Jesus openly received worship:

> "And they came into the house and saw the Child with Mary His mother; and they fell down and worshiped Him..." – Matthew 2:2.

Always Being Ready!

> "And when He again brings the first-born into the world, He says: 'And let all the angels of God worship Him.'" – Hebrews 1:6.

However, Jesus received more than worship, when, without rebuke in John 20:27-28, He was proclaimed by Thomas to be God. Instead of rebuking Thomas, which He should have done if this was not true, He said that all those who believed what Thomas believed would be blessed. One of the last things Jesus taught His disciples in His resurrection body was that He was God.

Christ's resurrection is vital because it confirmed our salvation [See for instance Acts 1:3 and Ephesians 1:19-20]. It also shows how we view the eternal nature of Christ and His ongoing heavenly ministry. The Christadelphians believe that Christ's resurrection was a physical one and that He has not changed since then.

> "It is suggested that Christ's nature was transformed into intangible essence after his ascension; but there is nothing to support such a suggestion ... no such change took place, and ... Christ ... continues to be the same real, though glorified, personage who exhibited his hands and feet to his assembled disciples."
> – *Christendom Astray*, Roberts, 1944, p.63.

> "... it is clear that the bodily resurrection of Christ from the dead always formed the central feature of the message." – *The Testimony*, October 1985, p.321

> "There is no doubt that Jesus rose bodily from the tomb... Only by his literal bodily presence were they convinced. This is resurrection - a literal bodily rising again to life." – *Resurrection and Judgement*, *Dawn* Booklet No.19, 1972, p.7.

What this means is that in heaven Christ just has a normal resurrection body as anyone else would have and He cannot fulfil His full heavenly ministry as God the Son. Whereas it is true that Christ rose physically, we are also made aware in Scripture that He has a glorified body in heaven. This body was released from the confines of His humanity so that He could fulfil His heavenly ministry as part of the Godhead. [See, for instance, Revelation 1:12-18.]

Many Christadelphians deny both the deity and personality of the *Holy Spirit*, claiming that He is not at work in this age:

> "He [Jesus] taught the personality of the Father, and of the son, but not of the Holy Spirit ... the Spirit is unseen power emanating from the Deity, filling all space, and by which he is everywhere present." – *The Real Christ*, J.J.Andrews, *The Dawn*, undated.

> "There is no manifestation of the Spirit in these days. The power of continuing the manifestation doubtless died with the apostles." – *Christendom Astray*, Roberts, 1944, p.99.

> "We may here remark that there is no scriptural authority whatever for regarding the Holy Spirit as the third person of a 'trinity'." – *The Holy Spirit*, *Dawn* Booklet No.4, 1971, p.10.

If you deny the work of the Holy Spirit, you also deny His ability to lead into all truth [see John 16:13]. Christadelphians have therefore placed much importance on their own writings:

> "We thank God that we are privileged to live in times when the Bible may be read in

> conjunction with the light thrown upon it by
> Eureka. ...We have only to try to imagine
> ourselves without this invaluable aid to the
> understanding not only of the Apocalypse,
> but also of the SCRIPTURES generally ...
> to realise how helpless our position would
> be." – *Light and Shade of the Truth's
> History, The Dawn,* undated, p.61.

The basic error lies in stating that the Spirit is not a person. It is clear from the Bible that He is power [see Luke 1:35] but the Scriptures also give conclusive evidence of His personality and deity. Jesus said of the Spirit,

> "I will pray the Father, and He shall give
> you another Comforter, that he may abide
> with you for ever." – John 14:16

W. E. Vine, in his *Expository Dictionary of New Testament Words,* points out that the Greek word for another in John 14:16:

> "... denotes another of the *same kind*." –
> Vine's *Dictionary of New Testament
> Words,* Vol.1, p.60. [Emphasis added.]

Christ is called the Advocate [1 John 2:1], the same Greek word as Comforter [John 14:16]. The One coming will be of the same kind as Christ; an impersonal force cannot fulfil this! The Holy Spirit is the Paraclete, meaning someone who went to court to speak for you. An impersonal force cannot do that!

The Christadelphians draw a distinction between 'The Spirit of God' and 'The Holy Spirit.' The first is the power of God, the basis of all things. The second is when that power is used for a specific purpose, for example, to guide and direct.

They also seek to explain away where Scripture says in one place that God does something and in another, the Holy Spirit does the same thing.

> "The difference between the Father and the Spirit, is only a difference from our point of view. ... The spirit is but the infinite extension, so to speak, of Himself; and when the spirit does anything, it is the Father doing it, because the spirit is not separate from the Father." – *Remember The Days Of Old*, A.Nicholls, 1977, p.42/3.

The Bible reveals that the Holy Spirit is distinct from the Father and the Son: for example John 14:16 and Acts 2:33. The Spirit is co-Creator [see among other verses Genesis 1:2-3, Psalm 33:6 and Job 26:13], yet, still God declares, He made all things, Isaiah 44:24 and 45:18. They are one, God the Father and God the Holy Spirit, both Deity and yet separate from each other.

Scripture gives further evidence of the deity of the Holy Spirit by attributing to Him the following qualities that are only found in God:

- He is eternal – Hebrews 9:14
- Omnipresent – Psalm 139:7-10
- Omnipotent – Luke 1:35 and Romans 15:13-19
- Omniscient – 1 Corinthians 2:10-11

When we accept the above teaching of the Christadelphians on the Father, Son and Holy Spirit, it is a natural assumption, of course, to deny *the Trinity*.

> "... Trinitarianism propounds – not a mystery but a contradiction – a stultification – an impossibility." – *Christendom Astray*, Roberts, 1944, p.89.

The one thing you cannot do is try to prove the doctrine of the Trinity with your mind, as you will never succeed. Define that the Trinity means that the Father, Son and the Holy Spirit are all God. Does the Bible show these three to be God? The answer is yes.

Always Being Ready!

We have dealt with some aspects of the Trinity in previous chapters but here are two Scriptures that we can use to show that the Trinity is taught within the Bible even if the word does not appear. First, several verses from John, chapter 1:

Verse 1 starts "In the beginning", the Greek phrase that is used in the Greek translation (Septuagint) for Genesis 1:1. There it had the meaning, "when the beginning began God was already there" and now here in John 1:1, "when the beginning began the Word, Christ, was already there." Neither of them created and both in existence before any creation took place. Hebrews 7:3 also shows that the Son of God had no "beginning of days or end of life": He is eternal.

John 1:3 states that *all* things were created by Him. The Word of God offers no exceptions as the emphasis in this verse shows: "apart from Him nothing came into being." Only if you bring human interpretation to bear can you say that Christ was a created being and not eternal.

John 8:58 is another clear declaration of the eternalness of Jesus. "Before Abraham was, 'I AM.'" Greek scholar A. T. Robertson, tells us about the Greek tense for I am:

> "The Progressive Present. This is a poor name in lieu of a better one for the present of a past action still in progress... In John 8:58 *eimi* is really absolute." – A *Grammar of the Greek New Testament in the Light of Historical Research*, p.879.

There is another interesting verse in John's gospel referring to John the Baptist, who, of course, was conceived and born before Jesus on this earth:

> "This is He on behalf of whom I said, 'After me comes a Man who has a higher rank than I, for He existed before me.'" - John 1:30

In this life Jesus never existed before John; He must therefore have existed as Jesus eternally.

Christadelphians believe that when man *dies* he is dead, unconscious and not knowing anything. Those who do not 'believe on' Jesus will simply cease to exist. Those who have believed will be **resurrected** with a tangible, incorruptible body that will not waste away or perish:

> "The record is devastatingly simple: death is not a door opening to a new life - it is a judgement for disobedience." – *After Death - What?*, F.Pearce, undated, p.6

> "The soul then, is the person, the living being. When he perishes, the soul, or life, perishes with him." – *Ibid.*, p.7

> "In view of the biblical evidence so far reviewed, it is no surprise to learn that the dead rest, completely unconscious in the grave." – *Ibid.*, p.7

A Biblical response to this doctrine could include the following:

Matthew 22:32 - departed saints are living and conscious with an immortal life that goes beyond the grave.

1 Thessalonians 5:10 - even if someone is asleep [the term used in Scripture of death] they are still alive in an immortal sense with Christ.

Matthew 10:28 - no one on earth can destroy the soul. Only God, Who created it, can destroy it, if it was His will. In other words, the soul is beyond the mortal; that is, it is immortal.

Luke 23:43, 2 Corinthians 5:1-8, and Philippians 1:23, all show that at death our soul is separated from the body and goes straight to be with the Lord.

Hebrews 12:23 shows that the spirits of the dead are already with the Lord.

For Christadelphians there is no *devil*:

> "... the popular doctrine of a personal devil has no foundation whatever in truth, but is

> the hideous conception of the heathen mind, inherited by the moderns from the mythologies of the ancients, and incorporated with Christianity by those 'men of corrupt minds' who, Paul predicted would pervert the truth 'giving heed to seducing spirits and doctrines of devils.'" – *Christendom Astray*, Roberts,
> The Christadelphian, 1944, p.118.

> "We know, of course, that there is no personal supernatural devil... It will be necessary... to demonstrate the falseness of the traditional belief that the devil is a superhuman being." – *The Devil the Great Deceiver*, Peter Watkins, 1976, p.13.

> "... by 'the devil' Paul means the sin-tendency which dwells in every member of the human race... 'Sin' which was condemned in the flesh of Jesus was the 'the devil' which it was his mission to overcome and destroy." – *God's Way*, John Carter, 1971, pp.139, 140.

Christadelphians seek to show how the names given to the evil one in Scripture are all manifestations within man himself. However, in John 13:27, we read, 'and after the sop, Satan entered into him'. Satan entered from the outside; he was not a manifestation within Judas.

1 Peter 5:8 is explained as persecution by the government but verse 9 tells them to, 'resist him'. James exhorts, 'resist the devil and he will flee'. Other passages to refer to include Luke 4:1-13 and Ephesians 6:12. Christ defeated the real enemy at Calvary by shedding His precious blood, Hebrews 2:14. He did not pay the ultimate sacrifice just for some ideas in man but we read:

> "The Son of God appeared for this purpose, that He might destroy the works of the devil." – 1 John 3:8.

Not ideas within a man but the outward works of the devil.

Heaven is not for man, according to the Christadelphian, and *hell* does not exist:

> "Heaven is God's abiding place... Man has no access into God's presence in heaven." – *Heaven and Hell*, D.Fifield, undated, pp.5-6
>
> "There are three main words in the Authorised Version which have been rendered 'Hell'. ... *Sheol* is therefore the grave, the common place of the dead where men's bodies are subject to decay. ... In the New Testament the word *hades* is the equivalent of the Hebrew *sheol* ... *gehenna*, a term always associated with fire. ... The reference to fires that are never quenched ... are used to express the nature of divine judgement ... nothing can prevent or interfere with the declared judgement of God upon those who turn their backs on him." – *Ibid.*, pp.7-9

There are a number of Scriptures that can be shared when seeking to show that this position is not a biblical one, these include:

Mark 9:43 - how is it better to be crippled in this life than to go off into annihilation? This only makes sense if we are talking about eternal punishment.

Matthew 25:46 uses the same word 'eternal' both for the punishment of the wicked and the life of the righteous. It must have the same meaning in both cases, i.e., lasting forever.

The Christadelphians will use the King James Bible and claim that they believe in the whole Bible, and have neither added nor taken away from it. However, the reality is quite different when you consider the verses that have been ignored or explained away to get the Bible to fit their theology.

Always Being Ready!

Sharing the gospel

Romans chapter 3 has some great verses to share. First, in verse 20, we read that by works no flesh will ever be justified. Being justified is that place, as Romans 5:1 explains, where we have peace with God. If we do not have peace with God when we die, there is no hope. The only way to have hope is to be justified (note Romans 5:1 says *having been* justified) and we are not justified by keeping commandments. Verse 23 shows that not one of us can make it to God's standard to be saved; we can only be saved by His grace, not by anything we do or not do.

In Ephesians 2:8-10, Paul makes a direct statement that it is by grace that we are saved, and then underlines three times that it has nothing to do with works or an attitude on my part at all. It is not of me - that is, it has nothing to do with me either flat-out works or seeking to obey commandments. It is God's gift freely given at the beginning and not taken back. Not because of works, else I could boast that I was saved because I kept the commandments. However, these verses do show us that there are works but we come into the good of them *after* we are saved and we work out the salvation we have received, not work to try to be good enough to pass Christ's judgement.

We also need to be aware that, if we live by the commandments, then we need to keep every single one of them all the time else judgement is ours:

> "For whoever keeps the whole law and yet stumbles in one point, he has become guilty of all." – James 2:10

Conclusion

A former Christadelphian suggested a great text to conclude with is John 5:39-40:

> "You search the Scriptures, because you think in them you have eternal life; and it is these that bear witness of Me; and you are unwilling to come to Me, that you may have life."

14 – Christian Science

Where did they come from?

The founder of Christian Science was Mary Baker Eddy. Born in 1821, the youngest of six children, she lived on a farm in the state of New Hampshire, USA. Her religious upbringing was that of a Congregationalist but during her teenage years she rejected their strong Calvinistic teachings.

Christian Science in many ways owes its existence to Mary's often poor health. This state is said to have caused her to question why the healings of Jesus were not manifest in her day. Seeking to find a human cure she was to experiment with homeopathy and hypnotism, among other alternatives, but nothing seemed to work.

Mary was first married when she was 22 but sadly her husband died after only seven months. The second marriage lasted longer but eventually it ended in divorce. Her third attempt at marriage was in 1877 to Asa Eddy who was to be her first disciple in Christian Science. However, it was during her second marriage in 1862 that she visited Phineas Quimby to find relief from her spinal illness. Quimby, who was to be involved in starting other cults such as Unity, used hypnosis and autosuggestion to bring healing. The man and his methods made an obvious impression on Mary and at one point she wrote to a local newspaper comparing Quimby to Jesus Christ.

Where the Church started

In 1866 she claimed healing from a serious injury that she was to declare later left her with only three days to live. The story goes that she was miraculously cured after reading Matthew 9:1-8, especially verse 2: "And behold, they were bringing to him a paralytic, lying on a bed; and Jesus seeing their faith said to the paralytic, 'Take courage, my son, your sins are forgiven.'"

Always Being Ready!

Looking back on the event it was not the physical healing that took on most significance. Rather, it was the awareness that she had received revelation of spiritual truths she had long searched for. She began to study for long hours and this led eventually in 1875 to her first publication, *Science and Health – with Key to the Scriptures*. Fifteen other writings would follow before her death. She claimed that *Science and Health* was her original study and that God was its author:

> "I would blush to write of Science and Health – with Key to the Scriptures as I have, were it of human origin and apart from God its author, but as I was only a scribe echoing the harmonies of Heaven in divine metaphysics, I cannot be super-modest of the Christian Science textbook."
> – *Christian Science Journal*, January 1901.

However, there is some evidence that it was taken from other sources such as Phineas Quimby and a German-American philosopher, Francis Lieber.

The first Christian Science church was founded in Boston, Mass, USA, on 12 April 1879. Today, their official web site claims that there are some 2,000 branches in 139 countries. They are all governed by the *Manual of the Mother Church*, first published in 1895.

Coming to the present day

Science and Health has now been translated into 17 different languages and English Braille. Official figures claim that it has sold ten million copies in all, with one million of these since 1996. Today, it is joined by such publications as *The Christian Science Journal* that was first published in 1883; *The Christian Science Quarterly* came next in 1890 and then in 1898 *The Christian Science Sentinel* appeared. Many will also be aware of their newspaper, *The Christian Science*

Monitor, which was first published in 1908. It has a daily edition in the USA, a weekly edition in 147 other countries and has recently been joined by a web and email edition. Apart from the written word, Christian Science has also over the years broadcast several radio and television programmes especially in the USA.

Financial problems

Modern-day financial problems have meant certain cutbacks and their monthly magazine *World Monitor* ceased to be published in May 1993. The project had only lasted five years and closed with reported losses of $36.5 million. This closure came on top of the cancellation of its cable television network.

The Annual General Meeting held on 8 June 1992 was dominated by two interrelated financial matters. First, the closure of the television cable channel at a cost of $68.5 million and second, the publication of a controversial book. Their president Nathan Talbot was aware of the problems when he told the assembly, "There are issues that would try and divide us. But ... the practice of spiritual healing binds us together."

Clearly there was a crisis among the Christian Scientists. The roots of this crisis could be found in the financial situation because they were losing $6,000,000 every month. This led on to an even deeper crisis of conscience.

Under the terms of a 1972 will, the church could inherit $97,000,000 if it published a book, *The Destiny of the Mother Church*, by Bliss Knapp, before April 1993. The problem was that many Christian Scientists believed that the book was heretical. They felt that it came very close to teaching that Mary Baker Eddy was a second Christ. She was described as God's 'original woman,' and Jesus was God's 'original man'. Whatever the struggle of conscience, the financial needs won and the book was published.

Always Being Ready!

Who are they?

Christian Science is reported to be losing ground in these days, with a 50% decline in practitioners in recent years. According to their own records, most of the members these days are American women.

Christian Science is neither Christian nor scientific. The central theme of its teachings is healing but with little scope for doctors or hospitals. Their philosophy is based on a mind-over-matter mentality. Many will sadly struggle with their illnesses and there are reported cases of tragic deaths because medical treatment is refused. I wonder how these people would react if they knew that Mary Baker Eddy in her lifetime could never prove one healing. She even had to turn to doctors at the end of her life, for a regular supply of morphine. Eddy indeed is the 'dying' proof that Christian Science is a fake. However, many who believe today will feel that they have a testimony of being 'healed' through the message of Christian Science. They will not want to hear anything to the contrary and will passionately believe that there is no other way.

What do they believe?

The tenets of their faith found in *Christian Science: A Report for the 90s*, p. 79, need to be read closely, because at first glance some may appear Christian:

1. As adherents of Truth, we take the inspired Word of the Bible as our sufficient guide to eternal life.

2. We acknowledge and adore one supreme and infinite God. We acknowledge His Son, one Christ; the Holy Ghost or divine Comforter; and man in God's image and likeness.

3. We acknowledge God's forgiveness of sin in the destruction of sin and the

spiritual understanding that casts out evil as unreal. But the belief in sin is punished so long as the belief lasts.

4. We acknowledge Jesus's atonement as the evidence of divine, efficacious Love, unfolding man's unity with God through Christ Jesus the Way-shower; and we acknowledge that man is saved through Christ, through Truth, Life and Love as demonstrated by the Galilean Prophet in healing the sick and overcoming sin and death.

5. We acknowledge that the crucifixion of Jesus and his resurrection served to uplift faith to understand eternal Life, even the allness of Soul, Spirit, and the nothingness of matter.

6. And we solemnly promise to watch, and pray for that Mind to be in us which was also in Christ Jesus, to do unto others as we would have them do unto us; and to be merciful, just, and pure.

Mary Baker Eddy's writings show that she believed that Christian Science was based on Scripture:

"The Bible has been my only authority. I have no other guide in 'the straight and narrow way' of Truth." – *Science and Health*, p. 126.

She considered that her writings were inspired: "No human pen nor tongue taught me the Science contained in this book" – *Science and Health*, p. 110. It is therefore no surprise that Christian Science seeks to go beyond the Bible and restore what was lost. It puts its own meaning into the Scriptures as the Lord's Prayer with spiritual interpretation by Eddy shows:

"Our Father which art in heaven.
Our Father-Mother God. all harmonious.
Hallowed be Thy name.
Adorable One.
Thy kingdom come.
Thy kingdom is come; Thou art ever-present.
Thy will be done in earth, as it is in heaven.
Enable us to know, as in heaven, so on earth. – God is omnipotent, supreme.
Give us this day our daily bread;
Give us grace for to-day; feed the famished affections;
And forgive us our debts, as we forgive our debtors.
And Love is reflected in love;
And lead us not into temptation, but deliver us from evil:
And God leadeth us not into temptation, but delivereth us from sin, disease, and death.
For Thine is the kingdom, and the power, and the glory, forever.
For God is infinite, all-power, all Life, Truth, Love, over all, and All." – Science and Health, pp. 16–17 quoted in *Christian Science: A Report for the 90s,* p. 78.

Their first tenet shows that they believe the **Bible** to be the sufficient guide to eternal life. But compare this with what Jesus said: "You search the Scriptures, because you think that in them you have eternal life; and it is these that bear witness of me." [John 5:39]. However, the report mentioned above, on page 40, shows clearly that Christian Scientists put *Science and Health* above the King James Version of the

Bible. *Science and Health* is the guide to the guide to eternal life and so more important:

> "These two books serve as the Church's pastor... People hungering for a better understanding of the Bible – yearning to see how it applies to today's world and to their own lives – find insight in *Science and Health*."

Mary Baker Eddy tried to say that her **God** was not pantheistic; that is, in everything, but her teaching shows the contrary:

> "(God is) The great I Am; the all-knowing, all-seeing, all acting. all-wise, all-loving and eternal: Principle; Mind; Soul: Spirit: Life: Truth; Love; all Substance; Intelligence." – *Science and Health*, p.587.

This pantheistic God also is evident in the last line of her interpretation of the Lord's Prayer shown above:

> "Christ is the ideal Truth, that comes to heal sickness and sin through Christian Science. Jesus is the name of the man who, more than all other men, has presented Christ, the true idea of God." – *Science and Health*, p. 473.

This 'Christ idea' or 'Christ consciousnesses' comes from eastern religions and appears in many New Age cults.

Eddy also makes it plain that **Jesus** is not God:

> "Jesus Christ is not God, as Jesus himself declared, but is the Son of God." – *Science and Health*, p. 361.

Always Being Ready!

She further claims that Jesus did not make full atonement for sin. Our effort is still needed:

> "Final deliverance from error ... not reached ... by pinning one's faith without works to another's vicarious effort. ... One sacrifice, however great, is insufficient to pay the debt of sin. The atonement requires constant self-immolation on the sinner's part. That God's wrath should be vented upon His beloved Son, is divinely unnatural. Such a theory is man-made." – *Science and Health.* pp. 22/23.

What is even more amazing is that Eddy goes on to tell us that Jesus did not really die!:

> "His disciples believed Jesus to be dead while he was hidden in the sepulchre, whereas he was alive, demonstrating within the narrow tomb the power of the Spirit to overrule mortal, material sense." – *Science and Health*, p. 44.

The cornerstone of Christian Science is healing and they alone have discovered the secret of Jesus' healing ministry:

> "Our Master ... practised Christian healing ... but left no definite rule for demonstrating this Principle of healing and preventing disease. This rule remained to be discovered by Christian Science." – *Science and Healing*, p. 147.

Many testimonies are published in various Christian Scientist magazines claiming miraculous recovery from illness. Some would appear genuine and this should not surprise us. The test of something is not whether it works, but where it comes from. There may be a 'power' in some of Christian Science but it certainly does not come from God, as their beliefs clearly show. They have another Jesus and another gospel.

Sin, sickness, death and hell are all unreal to the Christian Scientist. *Salvation* comes not from a relationship with Jesus Christ but from pretending the evil is not real. Hell is only the bad things within us and the effects of sin. (See *Science and Health*, p.588.):

> "... the only reality of sin, sickness, or death is the awful fact that unrealities seem real to human, erring belief, until God strips off their disguise." – *Science and Health*. p. 472.

Sharing the gospel

We have already mentioned the supposed belief of the Christian Scientist:

> "As adherents of Truth, we take the inspired Word of the Bible as our sufficient guide to eternal Life." – *Science and Health*, p. 497.

This is a good place to start because, if the Bible is the guide to eternal life, Mary Baker Eddy is the guide to hell. Ask them to compare the teachings of Eddy with the teachings of the Bible and choose which one to believe. Ask them why, if the Bible is the guide to eternal life, Eddy's beliefs are so different. Why indeed, when in some areas they are going in the opposite direction. Would that not mean that if we followed those beliefs we too would be going in the opposite direction to eternal life?

Some subjects that would be especially good to discuss are listed here with appropriate references.

The Bible clearly speaks of the reality of sin: Romans 3:23 and 1 John 1:8-10.

Always Being Ready!

The Bible shows the awful reality of Christ dying for the penalty of our sin: 2 Corinthians 5:21, 1 Peter 2:24 and 1 John 2:2.

God is shown to be separate from His creation; all is not one: Isaiah 44:24 and Acts 17:24-25.

Jesus and the Christ are shown to be the same person: Luke 2:11, 1 John 2:22 and 1 John 5:1.

Jesus both claimed to be and accepted the claim that He was God: John 5:18 and 20:28.

The Gospel expressly includes the death of Christ: 1 Corinthians 15:3.

15 – The International Churches of Christ

Who are they?

The denomination of the Churches of Christ has been in Britain for many years. The International Churches of Christ are a comparatively recent splinter group. The leaders of the established denomination have faced much frustration over the confusion that there is between themselves and the International Churches of Christ to the end that there has been the name change from the Central Church of Christ to the International Churches of Christ - UK. We use the abbreviation 'ICC' throughout this chapter but please note that, in a particular area, they would be known as the London International Churches of Christ or the Manchester International Churches of Christ, etc.

ICC, as far as Britain is concerned, was first based in London in 1982 and then spread to Birmingham and Manchester. In 2001, besides these three initial meetings, congregations were recorded in Cambridge, Coventry, Edinburgh, Cardiff, Glasgow, Leeds, Oxford and Southampton. The average Sunday attendance for all these places was 11,125 with 2,892 of these in London.

According to the official statistics of the ICC recorded at www.reveal.org/abouticc/iccstats.html, the number of recorded disciples on January 1 2001 was 2,798 and by 31 December 2001 it was, 2,764.

ICC in London was 'planted' by the Boston Central Church of Christ, Massachusetts, where the movement really developed. The founder was Kip McKean who had started his radical and revolutionary thinking at the 14th Street Church of Christ Gainesville while he was at the University of Florida. This church later changed its name to Crossroads Church of Christ. This 'Crossroads Philosophy', which is seen to be behind the ICC movement, is condemned by other Churches of Christ, including the elders at the original Crossroads fellowship. Kip McKean put it this way:

Always Being Ready!

> "Sadly, in time the leadership backed down on some of their convictions and innovations for the sake of remaining in 'fellowship' with all other elements of the modern Churches of Christ." - *Upside Down*, April 1992, p.7.

The activities of the Boston group also came in for severe criticism, especially on the local college campus. ICC rejected moves for reconciliation to the main churches at the end of 1990.

History

Most historians say that the "denomination" of the Church of Christ was founded in the early 1800s. Based on the idea that denominations were evil and there was only one true Church, Alexander Campbell, his father Thomas Campbell, Barton W. Stone and Walter Scott began teaching and preaching their message. Whereas this appears true from the evidence, some members of the Church of Christ would claim that they had been in existence much longer than that.

The 'Discipleship Movement' has influenced ICC. Not everything is wrong in this movement because there is a real teaching of discipleship but what is termed 'heavy shepherding', that is, domination, is wrong.

Some secular authorities have wanted to throw out 'the baby with the bath water', but we cannot do this. There are some Christians within the movement and some Christian principles in what they lay down. The mark they overstep is where instruction and encouragement become dictatorship and domination. For instance, one secular writer slates ICC for encouraging 'quiet times'. However, this is a very positive point - spending time getting to know the Lord. It is not the 'quiet time' that is wrong; only the attitude and manner in which it is taught.

Much of the blame for these wrong structures is put at the door of Robert Coleman's *The Master Plan of*

Evangelism. There is certainly ample evidence to show that the evangelistic thrust of ICC comes from this book.

The Memorial Church of Christ in Houston, Texas, originally supported Kip McKean along with Roger Lamb. When they started teaching what were felt to be wrong doctrines, the support was withdrawn. McKean and Lamb said that their method of delivering the message came from Coleman's book.

Yet, what is also clear is that most of the doctrines they are so evangelistic about were already inherent within the Church of Christ. The complaints and split are mainly concerning method and emphasis.

The thrust of 'heavy discipleship' coming from Coleman's book can be summed up in the following excerpts:

> "make leaders . . . not simply mere followers." – p.109

> "All of this is going to require a lot of supervision... Carnal attitudes and reactions need to be detected early and dealt with decisively ..." – p.123

> "As their guardian and advisor we are responsible for teaching our spiritual children ..." – p.124

The thrust for total obedience is seen in:

> "They were not required to be smart but they had to be loyal... nor will he sincerely take the step of faith unless he is willing to obey what his leader says." – p.50

Even though Kip McKean was the founding influence, he has now resigned. He had run the church with a rule of authority that in the end led to his downfall. He had taught that no one could be a leader if their children left the ICC, and that's just what his daughter did.

Always Being Ready!

Farah Stockman reported in the *Boston Globe* in May 2003:

> "'I'm convinced,' McKean told followers in Washington, D.C., in 2000, 'that when a teen falls away [from the church] ... there are some sinful dynamics in that family, and that family, that mom and dad, need to repent.'
>
> "But Olivia had just left for Harvard University, and she was already tasting the freedom of life away from home. For a while, she attended the Boston Church of Christ and even gave dynamic speeches to crowds of hundreds. Although the church paid for her discipler, a young woman from Los Angeles, to move to Cambridge with her to guide her spiritual growth, by January 2001, Olivia stopped coming to church and told her friends she no longer wanted to be a member.
>
> "'She finally just stood up and said, "I'm sick of the whole thing; I'm leaving",' said one former church leader who knew her personally. Her father 'was pretty brokenhearted.'"

McKean's resignation letter began:

> "Truly the Lord has blessed his modern day movement as His gospel has produced true churches of disciples in nearly 170 nations over the past 23 years."

This particular phrase and further on in the letter where he calls the movement, 'the Kingdom', shows that he still believes that this movement is the Lord's modern day movement to the exclusion of others.

The letter also indicates that he feels that he is personally at fault but that the movement as a whole needs little change to the way it has been going.

International Churches of Christ

The statement put out by the new leadership informed us:

> "The responsibility of the Unity Meeting and conference would be to make sure that we remain cooperative and unified while we continue the task of evangelizing our various sectors of the world."

In other words, there would still be a central leadership from Los Angeles that would filter its way through to every ICC church worldwide.

Britain is going through a major crisis, as an open letter dated February 2003 from Henry Kriete shows. Kriete is still a member of ICC in Britain:

> "As many of you know, in London we are in the midst of a spiritual upheaval. I would even call it a crisis or an unravelling. Please continue in your prayers for us. The London and UK churches have had an incredible history and as a movement we owe them much. Unfortunately, over the years, because of harshness and legalism and systemic problems I will soon identify, the churches have suffered dearly."

The future of the church is clearly in the balance and the article by *Christianity Today*, June 2003, which takes up the Kriete letter, seems to sum up the current situation:

> "'Boston Movement' Apologizes Open letter prompts leaders of controversial church to promise reform. By John W. Kennedy - posted 06/04/2003
> "A London leader's 39-page confessional open letter detailing abuses in the International Churches of Christ (ICOC)

has further shaken a movement that has been controversial since its beginning 24 years ago. Whether the movement, an offshoot of the mainline Churches of Christ and known for its aggressive campus recruiting, is unravelling or reforming is hard to say.

"The February 2 letter followed the resignation of founder Kip McKean in November (CT, March 2003, p. 26). Evangelist Henry Kriete, an influential leader in the Boston Movement (the informal name of the ICOC) in six countries and ten churches, wrote the letter. Kriete said the ICOC's viability was at stake. He said leaders have engaged in financial mismanagement, legalism, dishonest statistical reporting, and abusive teachings, and have ignored critics."

Unravelling or reforming seems to be the question; we will need to wait to find out the answer.

Beliefs

We quote from ICC's initial bible study in *Guard the Gospel*. This was reprinted in a slightly revised form, in their book *Shining Like Stars*. This shows beyond doubt the cultic tendencies of the group.

These studies came out of Kip Mckean's early series of Bible studies:

"Early on I developed a series consisting of nine Bible studies on the 'first principles'. ... The members of the church were called to memorize these studies and then teach others to become Christians. The most impacting was called 'Discipleship' where

> ... I taught ... SAVED = CHRISTIAN = DISCIPLE, simply meaning that you cannot be saved and you cannot be a true Christian without being a disciple also. I purposely developed this study to draw sharp biblical distinction between the ... Boston Church of Christ and all other groups." – *Upside Down*, April 1992, p.7.

Baptism - essential for salvation

> "LESSON 5... OBJECTIVES - to show that 1. Baptism is essential for salvation ... Paul's sins were washed away only after he was baptised."

Kip McKean develops this further:

> "I taught that to be baptized, you must first make a decision to be a disciple and then be baptized. I saw that people in and outside of our fellowship had been baptized without this understanding and then, in time, developed a disciple's commitment to make Jesus Lord of their entire life. I taught that their baptism was invalid because a retroactive understanding of repentance and baptism was not consistent with Scripture. Upon conviction by the Scriptures, most people... were rebaptized." – *Upside Down*, April 1992, pp.7, 8

Baptism is a very important act and we are commanded to be baptised - this is not in question. The question we need to answer is: Does the Bible show that baptism is essential for me to be saved, or does it follow salvation as a testimony to what has happened?

Always Being Ready!

Please note that the verses that the ICC uses have already been discussed and answered on page 135 and we will not repeat this here.

There are, however, some verses that ICC admits are problems [see *Shining Like Stars*, pp.289, 290]. These are ones therefore that are good to use in talking with members of the group. Luke 23:43 - when did the thief on the cross receive baptism? Romans 10:9-10, 13 and John 3:16 that are both clear promises of salvation without baptism. If God is not true to His Word, then I cannot rely on Him at all!

Holy Spirit

> "The Holy Spirit. Definition: God's (personal) presence. ... Received at baptism. ... Hence necessary for salvation ... since the Cornelius incident, there has been no Holy Spirit Baptism ... there are no gifts of the Holy Spirit today."

Acts 2:38-39. These verses go way beyond the 120 in the upper room and still apply for us today.

Ephesians 5:18. Be being filled with the Spirit - continuous.

1 Corinthians 13:10. Gifts are only partial, not the fullness. They reveal God to us in this world now. However, when that which is perfect - the Kingdom of God - is come fully they will pass away. The gifts remain until then.

Salvation

> "FALSE DOCTRINES PERTAINING TO CONVERSION ... salvation by 'faith alone' ... salvation by 'praying Jesus into your heart' (sometimes termed 'accepting Christ'). ... 'Once Saved, Always Saved.'"

Ephesians 2:8-10: By grace you have been saved, [past tense], through faith that is the gift of God. This has nothing to do with works. After being saved, we walk in the works that we were created for.

James 2:14: This passage is talking to brethren, those who have been saved. Now walk in works prepared.

Verse 22 tells us that faith is perfected by works. Faith does not come through works but they ensure that faith can be seen.

Verse 26 shows that the body is in existence even without spirit, but there is no action. The faith that is within a person is not full until it is expressed.

Phillippians 2:12: We do not work towards salvation, but we work out what we have already received. NB v.13: God is at work in you.

Matthew 24:13. This does not say, if we do not endure we will lose eternal life. Compare Luke 21:18,19, where in the same context it talks about not a hair of your head will perish. We may indeed lose physical life but not spiritual.

Hebrews 6:6. Verse 8 tells us that they come close to being cursed and burned. See 1 Corinthians 3 below in this context.

Hebrews 10:26: The key here is sinning wilfully.

1 Corinthians 3:12-15. There are two possible types of building material. The first is that which man builds and this is made of wood, hay and stubble that will pass away. The second is God's, of gold, silver and precious stones, which are of eternal value. Verse 4 shows that there is a reward for doing God's works but it is not being born again. Salvation is separate from man's works. All works can go but salvation is still there.

Other Doctrines

> "The majority of churchgoers have never repented."

This leads to a vigorous evangelising of these very churchgoers:

Always Being Ready!

> "Be personally involved in one another's lives, lest sin cause anyone to forfeit his/her salvation . . . daily contact - must persevere to the very end (no 'once saved, always saved')."

This leads to an over-emphasis on discipleship:

> "Come to all the services... Be supportive of leadership - follow them as they follow Christ... relationships with the people we are closest to must not get in the way."

This leads to the conclusion that ICC's meetings are vital. You must obey the leadership without question and cut off your old family ties.

Members of ICC will use a regular *Bible* but, as we have shown, they will take verses out of context to make them fit their own beliefs.

Sharing the gospel

Many in ICC will already have a personal relationship with Jesus. For such our primary aim is probably to show them the cultic tendency to claim that their church is the only one that can really bring salvation. If we can lead them away from ICC they will not then be stumbling others with their false doctrine and will be able to grow properly in the Christian life.

For those who do not have a personal relationship with Jesus share with them that it is not the outward acts, baptism, bible reading, hours of prayer, etc., that save, but knowing Jesus [John 5:39,49]. Share the grace of the Lord Jesus Christ [2 Corinthians 8:9, Ephesians 2:8-10] and passages concerning His friendship and love [John 15:13-15].

Conclusion

What do you do when you come to the end of a book like this? Put it on the shelf and forget it? Make a mental note that one day you must do something about it? I hope that you will not just put off the decision but be encouraged to put the lessons of this book into practice straight away.

There is a mission field waiting for you, and it is not in some remote part of the globe. The challenge is of the cults on your doorstep or in your High Street. If you have had difficulty in getting people interested in the gospel in your area, you should praise the Lord for the cults. Their members are not apathetic like so many you meet; most are already aware of their need for a spiritual input. We can simply turn that to our advantage in communicating the gospel.

First, I am aware that I have not answered every question but, as we are a ministry, you are very welcome to write to us with further queries. Any subjects that we have raised that you do not understand or areas that are not clear, please contact us at:

Reachout Trust
24 Ormond Road
Richmond
Surrey TW10 6TH

Phone 0870 770 3258
Fax 0870 770 3259

Email: rt@reachouttrust.org
Web: http://www.reachouttrust.org

We may not be able to deal with every enquiry immediately, but we will gladly answer any questions and provide further literature specifically designed to help you be ready to reach out to the cults in your area.

Always Being Ready!

Second, I want to give you just a few ideas of what you can do so that you will not be just a hearer but a doer also.

You can be what I call a passive witness. This is where you take the lessons of this book to heart and get prepared. Then when the knock comes on the door or you meet the cult member in the High Street, you spring into action. I pray that everyone who reads this book will at least go as far as that.

I am hoping that a number will take this further and become active witnesses. Here, we will not be just waiting for the cult members to come to us, but will be looking for ways to contact them directly. Possibilities for achieving this are advertisements in shop windows, newspapers, etc. It will mean that you will not only contact those in the cults but also those beginning to study with them. People in the latter category are very important because prevention is better than cure. In other words it is easier to show people it is wrong to go into the cult than to try to bring them out after many years. Hardly a week goes by at the office without two or three people of this kind contacting us. What is even better is that many find the true Saviour instead of the false gospel of the cults.

Another way that you can reach out is by arranging to deliver warning tracts in your neighbourhood. Beyond this you may want to be available to help others in the churches in your area to be ready to share their faith with cult members.

At Reachout Trust we want to hear from you, whatever your decision is concerning the message in this book. We would very much like to know what your conclusions are and why you have arrived at them because this will help us in our future work.

Finally, I want to say again that I hope that many of you will be encouraged and motivated to build bridges of love to those in the cults that are all around you, and that we are here to help you in whatever way we can.

Further details of many of these groups can be found on the Reachout Trust website.

Guide to Helpful Materials

Most of these resources are available from Reachout Trust. Request a copy of our complete catalogue from the address on p.213 or download a copy from our web site - http://www.reachouttrust.org/downloads/Resource.pdf. You can also order most resources direct from our web site shop - http://www.reachouttrust.org and follow the links to 'purchases'.

Jehovah's Witness

The Jehovah's Witnesses - Their Beliefs and Practices - D.Harris
Detailed information and teaching

A Look Into Jehovah's Witnesses - Reachout Trust
Overview information and teaching

Jehovah's Witness Teaching Notes - Reachout Trust
Detailed information and teaching

Why Should You Believe ... Trinity? - Doug Harris
Testimony

Examining the Watchtower Bible - Reachout Trust
Overview information and teaching

Reasoning from the Scriptures - Ron Rhodes
Detailed information and teaching

Jesus of Nazareth - Who Is He? - Arthur Wallis
Detailed information and teaching

Reach Out to Jehovah's Witnesses
Video - documentary style

Awake! to the Watchtower
Double video teaching set

Mormons

Mormonism A Gold Plated Religion - Mike & Ann Thomas
Detailed information and teaching

Mormon Teaching Notes - Mike & Ann Thomas
Detailed information and teaching

Always Being Ready!

A Look Into the Mormons - Doug Harris
Overview information and teaching

Reasoning From the Scriptures - Ron Rhodes
Detailed information and teaching

Mormonism 101 - Bill McKeever / Eric Johnson
Detailed information and teaching

Mormonism - A Gold Plated Religion
Video - documentary style

.DNA vs The Book of Mormon
Video or DVD - documentary style

The Bible and The Book of Mormon
DVD- documentary style

The Lost Book of Abraham
DVD- documentary style

Christadelphians

A Look Into the Christadelphians - Doug Harris
Overview information and teaching

General

Cults and More - Doug Harris
Overview information and teaching on the groups mentioned in this book plus more.

Should Christians Apologise? - Reachout Trust
Detailed information and teaching on apologetics

Reasoned Defence Pack - Reachout Trust
Answers to ten 'hard-to-explain' questions

Evidence that Demands a Verdict - Josh McDowell
Detailed information and teaching on apologetics

The Trinity - Rose Publications
Overview information and teaching

On our website, you will also find other Fact Files and notes covering, in more detail, some of the groups mentioned in this book, plus other groups not mentioned.

Index - Subject

Index - Scriptures

Index

Always Being Ready!

Always Being Ready!

Printed in the United Kingdom
by Lightning Source UK Ltd.
108787UKS00001B/67-216